WHY I AM

AN EPISCOPALIAN

By JOHN MCGILL KRUMM

Roadblocks to Faith, with Dean James A. Pike, 1954

WHY I AM
AN EPISCOPALIAN

By

John McGill Krumm

THOMAS NELSON & SONS

EDINBURGH   NEW YORK   TORONTO

TO

GEORGE EDWARD SWAN, *Priest and Doctor*
STEPHEN CUTTER CLARK, *Bishop and Doctor*
W. BERTRAND STEVENS, *Bishop and Doctor*

INSPIRING EXEMPLARS, IN THE VARIETY OF THEIR
GIFTS AND PERSONALITIES, OF ANGLICAN CHRISTIANITY

CONTENTS

INTRODUCTION

AT the university where I now minister as Chaplain
every entering student is invited to state what our
registration form refers to as a "religious preference." It
is interesting to speculate as to what that phrase "religious
preference" really means. How have most of us arrived at
the particular spiritual household where we now abide?
The term "religious preference" may be misleading if it
suggests that we have carefully examined all the possible
religious alternatives and then made a judicious selection
based on our own taste and temperament or on the inherent
persuasiveness of the religious position itself. Such a meaning for "religious preference" is misleading because this is
not at all the way in which most of us have found our way
into our religious affiliation.

As a matter of fact, many students at my university state
as their religious preference the affiliation of their parents,
and they do not mean to imply that they have given this

9

affiliation any very careful scrutiny. Even those who have formed an ecclesiastical or religious connection with some show of independence will admit that all kinds of circumstantial factors have played a major part in their action. A chance acquaintance with some minister, the invitation of a friend or neighbor, the convenient location or attractive appearance of some church building—these are the factors which many of us would confess had most to do with our "religious preference." To an outsider all this will appear to be mere happenstance. If I had not moved to a certain town, known a certain friend, met a certain minister, I would not be an Episcopalian at all, all of the supposedly weighty arguments of this little book notwithstanding.

Because, however, these apparently arbitrary personal experiences have led to the apprehension of deeply significant truth, the believer can never put them down to mere luck or chance. We shall always say with St. Paul, "By the grace of God, I am what I am." So while I must confess that I became a Christian within the fold of the Episcopal Church and the Anglican Communion through a series of personal experiences of a seemingly arbitrary sort, I must also insist that I remain an Episcopalian gladly and enthusiastically because in and through these personal experiences the Spirit Himself has led me to profound and persuasive truth.

So this little book will have two parts. First, a brief telling of a series of events which brought me into the Episcopal Church and kept me there. This constitutes the first chapter of the book. More important is the description of what the Episcopal Church has come to mean to me, how it appears to me to combine in one inclusive formulation of faith and experience so many aspects of the truth about God and man and their relationship one with another. It would, of course, be quite out of keeping with the spirit and intention of this series to make disparaging or invidious comparison between my own Church and other communions and fellowships. At the same time, I must plainly warn the reader that I do not consider religious connection and association to be merely a matter of taste, much as some people prefer black olives and other people green. Ultimately I am an Episcopalian not because it suits me, for it does not always do so exactly and indeed sometimes irritates me very much indeed. I am an Episcopalian ultimately because I believe that in this Church and Communion the great truth of Christianity is most adequately and fully set forth in balance and proportion and that through its life of worship and witness it makes possible the richest kind of fellowship with God and with fellowmen. That I was drawn to this Church I regard as the leading of a gracious and provident God, and I am glad to be able to try to tell what He taught me and showed me in this experience.

WHY I AM

AN EPISCOPALIAN

ONE

VITA SUA

IT IS NOT too far from the truth to say that I am an
Episcopalian because I was bribed into being one! It was
a persuasive proposition put to me by my friend down the
street who had joined the ranks of a newly launched boys'
choir in the Episcopal Church in the California town
where I lived. I was twelve years old, and the choir needed
recruits. Whether my friend was authorized to put the
matter to me in just the way he did I now have some doubt.
His method was nevertheless successful—indeed, far beyond
his expectations. The choir was due to make its debut on
Christmas Eve. Then as a reward for the long weeks of
preparation and rehearsal its members were to be taken
shortly after Christmas for a visit to San Francisco, some
four hundred miles away, for a glamorous visit to China-
town and kindred delights. What could be simpler, my
friend insisted, than to spend a few weeks practicing hymns
and anthems, join the Christmas debut and the subsequent

San Francisco excursion and then shake the dust of the
Episcopal Church off my feet as soon afterwards as decency
would permit?

I was free to turn this proposition over in my mind without any religious prejudices or commitments to interfere
with its full consideration. I had grown up in a home
which both my parents then and I now would insist on
describing as a Christian home in many important ways.
It was not, however, a home marked by specifically religious
practices of any kind. I can never remember that we said
grace before meals, joined in family prayers, or ever attended church together as a family group.

My father's family were devout members of the Lutheran
Church, Missouri Synod, and in that church I was baptized
shortly after birth. In fulfillment of the baptismal promises,
my parents undertook to send me to the Lutheran Sunday
School. The subsequent failure of that attempt had nothing
whatever to do with the liturgical or theological standards
of the Lutheran Church, a great Communion for which in
my adult life I have come to have the highest respect and
a warm sense of kinship. The plain truth was that the
Missouri Synod Lutherans of that particular parish had
learned very little about how to attract or win children's
attention and interest. My recollection of the Sunday
School classroom was a bare and unattractive room—the
predominant color being a dirty gray—in which we sat in
stiff wooden chairs that were too big for us, making an
effort to remember what Luther said in his *Small Catechism*
was the meaning of the Ten Commandments or of the
Apostles' Creed. I dimly recall one day when we were permitted to go into the church building itself for some kind

of special service. It was an exciting and mysterious place, with what seemed vast and dim and soaring spaces which made an unforgettable impression upon me. Next Sunday, however, we were back in the Sunday School classroom with Dr. Luther's catechism, and I found nothing very exciting, I am sorry to say, about that.

My career as a Lutheran was interrupted by an appeal from some neighborhood children to go to the Methodist Sunday School with them, and perhaps because it was closer and easier to get to, I went. It seemed a much more pleasant place, and I was flattered to be asked to take part in a church pageant in the role of the lad with the barley loaves and fishes. When we moved to California there was no Missouri Synod Lutheran Church in the town where we settled, and I visited about, carried hither and thither by the appeals of friends, the attractive personalities of teachers and pastors, and the practical exigencies of convenience of location. I had achieved some fame in the local Methodist Sunday School by giving a chalk talk on the love of money being the root of all evil, but I was essentially adrift as far as religion was concerned when the Episcopal Church appeared on the horizon in the guise of my friend's rather cynical appeal. I accepted.

The weeks of rehearsal went by, and I found I really liked to sing. The hymn tunes were attractive and memorable. It was fun trying to figure out the intricacies of Anglican chanting—a kind of secret cabalism, the mastery of which gave me a delightful sense of being inside an exclusive fraternity. (I am afraid it gives just the impression of being "outside" to the average visitor to Episcopal services of worship!) Being fitted for vestments was also exciting, for I liked the idea of getting "dressed up" and promptly went off with my friend and got photographed in vestments for a Christmas gift to my parents. It did not then occur to me that this photograph might constitute a hostage to fortune and would mock me later if I persisted in my intention of an early post-Christmas desertion! Then, however, came Christmas Eve itself, and I was entranced. The Christmas greens and the yellow candles, the dignity and reverence of the service, and the sense of being an important part of a great significant activity—all this captivated me completely. Somehow the San Francisco trip had become a little vague anyway in all the weeks of rehearsal, but that didn't trouble me at all. I never got to San Francisco under these auspices, but I got somewhere much more important. I had found a spiritual home, and I knew it.

In a few weeks I had broken my ties with the Methodist Sunday School—even though flattering vistas of more chalk talks beckoned—and was enrolled in the Episcopal Sunday School. Soon it was announced that the Bishop was coming for Confirmation in the spring when the fine new church building was going to be opened and dedicated. One afternoon when I came home from school I found the rector's car parked in front of my house, and when I went inside he was asking my mother whether she thought I was interested in being confirmed. Of course, I was, and went every week to Confirmation classes. I cannot remember very much about the instruction. My "conversion" was not at that moment predominantly (or even at all) a theological one. The rector, however, said one thing that took a great burden off my mind. He was discussing the Apostles' Creed and the phrase, "Creator of Heaven and earth." "To believe this does not mean that we are not free to accept all the discoveries of modern science," he said. "It may be that the evolutionary theory will be found to be true, and if so we are bound to accept it. The Creed is not interested in telling us how the world was created, but only that God was behind it all." These classes took place the same year that the Scopes trial was held in Dayton, Tennessee, and this simple observation of the rector was a great illumination and relief to me.

The rector also reminded us that when the Bishop laid his hands on our heads in the Confirmation service, he would be repeating what had been done to him in his own Confirmation, Ordination and Consecration, and that in turn the Bishops who had laid their hands on his head had also been received into the Church and into the ministry in the same way. There was no hard theological point made of all this, but it gave one the sense of participation in a great historical movement. I looked forward to the Bishop's coming with the unconscious feeling that he was the symbol and focus of a rich and age-old tradition into which I was being initiated. The Bishop indeed looked the part. He was a striking and handsome man with piercing eyes and a magnificent and rich voice. As I heard him rumbling down the line of kneeling candidates, approaching me as I knelt at the altar rail, I was deeply aware of the important decision I had made and of the dignified and ancient heritage into which I was entering.

My family's move to another town made it necessary to transfer my membership to a new parish, but my religious commitment survived the transplanting. Soon I was deeply involved in all the activities of another parish, this one a typically busy and energetic one. I grew up through the high school and college years as an acolyte, Sunday School teacher, lay reader, an officer in the youth organization. This particular parish was committed to an unusually serious program of Christian education and drew into itself a remarkable group of professionally competent educators. The community in which it was placed had a deservedly high reputation for the excellence of its public schools, and the rector skilfully marshalled these resources of his community for the Church's educational task. I was enrolled as a Sunday School teacher, and at our weekly staff meetings we debated educational theory and practice with the Sunday School classroom as our laboratory. I cannot imagine many teachers' colleges which could offer more stimulating educational experience.

One Sunday afternoon after dinner in the rectory, the rector drew me aside in his study for a talk. What was I planning to do as a life vocation? Had I ever thought of entering the ministry? Of course, I had, but I felt appalled at the spiritual demands which such a vocation would entail, and was much more inclined to continue my studies in history, which I greatly enjoyed, and to look forward to a career as a teacher. I had never known any great mystical experiences, and I supposed something of this sort was a requirement for the ministry. To my surprise the rector confessed that he had never known any such dazzling or overwhelming experiences either. He advised me to read some biographies of prominent clergymen and also a little book on the ministry by the Rt. Rev. Charles L. Slattery. One point in the little book may very well have been decisive. At any rate I can remember it twenty-five years later. Bishop Slattery insisted that the Church's ministry could use any talent or combination of talents a man possessed. Business and administrative skill, literary and artistic talents, intellectual power, sociability and an intuition in dealing with people—all these and any other gifts a man possessed were useful for the ministry of the Church of God. This idea struck me with great force. There was not only one kind of ministry, but each man could bring his peculiar gifts to the task. The rector advised me to think it over and not to commit myself until I was sure. Before my junior year in college, I went to see the Bishop and was formally accepted by him as a Postulant for Holy Orders.

My last two years of college were spent at a great state university, the University of California at Los Angeles. At the Bishop's suggestion I changed my major from history to philosophy and was soon plunged into the kind of stimulating and exciting intellectual crisis that a college education at its best ought to provide. Two men made deep impressions—one negative and one positive. A course in ethics was brilliantly taught by a religiously skeptical pragmatist. From him I learned, in the words of California's President, Robert Gordon Sproul, to ask two questions of any proposition: "Is it true?" and "What of it?" My religion had to make a difference in attitudes and behavior if it was to mean anything to me. To this extent I was a pragmatist. I was prepared to be radical in my treatment of the Christian tradition, if necessary, focusing it on what I thought was the major human problem—namely, social reconstruction. How I struggled through that year with the skepticism of this stimulating teacher!

The other major influence was a professor of meta-
physics, Scandinavian in origin, with a charm and a sweet-
ness that were irresistible. His poetic skill gave to his
lectures and writings a beauty and a power that lifted his
courses to the level of a genuine religious experience. He
was mainly concerned with cosmology, and, making use of
Plato (especially portions of the *Timaeus*), he gave us an
unforgettable picture of the creator God brooding over
the chaos of the world, ever working to bring it to beauty
and truth and goodness. As a result of this course in meta-
physics, I was convinced, despite my skeptical professor of
ethics, that it *was* intellectually respectable to be a Christian and to talk and think about God. A cosmology in
which God was seeking higher levels of goodness and order
fitted in also with my growing interest in social reconstruction and gave it setting and depth.

During my college years we were in the midst of the
"Great Depression," and it had touched my own family
and affected us seriously. More than that, it had taken
everywhere an obvious toll in human dignity. Men reduced
to meaningless and unproductive work felt deeply the loss
of status and the implied discounting of their significance.
My own grandfather, who had worked all his life as a
foreman of a paint shop in a large industrial plant and had
retired on a pension, found his life's savings wiped out and
his pension snatched away by the company's being sold
without any pension guarantees required. As a consequence he went back to work as a day laborer at the age
of 72. We burned with indignation at the kind of society
that allowed this sort of thing—and many things much
worse—to happen to human beings. The promise of a "new

deal" seemed a summons to a great campaign to right ancient wrongs and provide a more secure and just society.

My concern was with the Church's role in this revolution. Could the ethics of the New Testament say something to this situation? I was cheered and encouraged by
the Church's response to the challenge. I read eagerly
about the Church League for Industrial Democracy and
later in my seminary days joined it and attended its meetings. The stirring Pastoral Letters issued during those
years by the House of Bishops impressed me deeply, especially the call of the Davenport Pastoral of 1933 for a cooperative industrial order and for the renunciation of war.
My heroes were Bishop Edward L. Parsons of California,
Suffragan Bishop Robert B. Gooden of Los Angeles, and
Suffragan Bishop Charles K. Gilbert of New York.

I taught a Sunday School course during my college days
which dealt with the Hebrew Prophets, and I can remember leading a discussion on what Amos would say if he
were to speak over a microphone in the Los Angeles Col-
iseum. It was during the time of a bitter street-car strike,
and some of the parents of my Sunday School pupils complained to the rector about my easy identification of social
righteousness with the cause of the striking employees. On
another occasion, I was asked to address the Corporate
Communion of the Diocese held each year for men and
boys on the occasion of George Washington's Birthday.
My argument was roughly that just as George Washington
had to fight for political freedom in his time, so in our
time the summons was to struggle for industrial freedom
for the laboring classes. I used for illustration the bitter
strike of the migrant farm workers in the Imperial Valley.

The reaction of the audience, I now suppose, was that of indulgence of this rather wild-eyed college student. What was more significant to me at the time was the sympathy and encouragement that I got after outbursts like this from some of the clergy and bishops.

As I entered the seminary, I am afraid that my view was that the Episcopal Church, while it was somewhat cumbersome and slow in its operations, might under my expert methods of reform and reconstruction become a useful agency for social transformation! The brashness and unrealism of this view now seem to me abundantly clear, but at the time it served to reinforce and sustain my interest in the Church and in the ministry. My theology was that of the social Gospel movement in its more naive form. I was a convinced pacifist and socialist. I knew that I was in the minority in the Episcopal Church in these convictions, but I was encouraged by the knowledge that some of its leaders, at any rate, shared them with me. My purpose in going to seminary was to acquire the necessary technical knowledge that would enable me to operate a parish and to satisfy the ordination requirements. In this supremely self-satisfied and self-confident mood, I entered the Virginia Theological Seminary in the fall of 1935. To use an expressive current slang phrase, the Seminary "had news for me."

It was only in the Virginia Seminary that the Episcopal Church's theological tradition began to reach me and to influence me. More than that, it ushered me into a surprisingly wonderful experience of fellowship in prayer and study. Being somewhat isolated in its semi-rural setting, the Seminary had developed a unique sense of community of its own. The homes of the faculty were located on the spacious seminary grounds and we enjoyed a singularly happy and contented community life. Throughout its more than one hundred years of history the Virginia Seminary had developed a deeply Evangelical tradition within the Episcopal Church. The emphasis was on simplicity in ritual and ceremony—indeed it seemed almost too bare and austere for my taste—and great importance was given to the reality of personal religion, especially private prayer. The so-called "faculty meetings," which were, as a matter of fact, more like an old-fashioned prayer meeting, were occasions once each week for an address by a faculty member on a topic of devotional interest, accompanied by acts of prayer and intercession. Each evening in our dormitories someone of the students led what were called "hall prayers" in his room, and most of the students made it a habit to come. Occasional Quiet Days were also held, and we had frequent opportunites to hear the professors and fellow students preach in chapel. It was a far richer, more concentrated spiritual fare than I had ever known or anticipated. Slowly and gradually it served to deepen my own religious concern and to broaden the meaning of the Christian religion for me.

Theologically the Seminary was, of course, my "great awakening." I arrived in the midst of a kind of interim period in the development of the Seminary itself. W. Cosby Bell had been a great professor of theology and had molded a generation of students in a distinctly liberal fashion. His memory was still evoked on occasions, but there was no doubt that a new kind of spirit and attitude was beginning to be felt. Charles W. Lowry was teaching theology, bringing to it a vast and impressive historical knowledge, but

more exciting and formative for me was the influence of
Albert T. Mollegen. Professor Mollegen had come to the
Seminary fresh from graduate work at Union Theological
Seminary and plunged us at once into the thought of what
has come to be called "neo-orthodoxy." I had already in my
last year in college read Walter Marshall Horton's *Realistic
Theology,* which brought me up sharp with its suggestions
that ideas such as sin and salvation had a deeper significance than had usually been ascribed to them in the liberal
social Gospel tradition.

World events, of course, also conspired to force any
Christian who had been living on the basis of a liberal
social Gospel theology to probe somewhat more deeply.
The kind of social reconstruction that had been so enthusiastically undertaken under the auspices of the New Deal
appeared wholly irrelevant and helpless in the face of the
rising menace of Nazism. Here was the reality of sin and
evil focused with an intensity and power that would not
yield to any simple moralism even of a socialistic or paci-
fistic variety. The meaning of what was taking place in
the world around us was daily brought home to us in our
theological studies. We heard Hitler raving over the radio
at a Nazi rally one day, and the next we were exegeting a
passage from the Epistle to the Ephesians concerning "spiritual wickedness in high places."

My earlier confidence with its attending patronizing attitude toward the Church and its theological traditions now
gave way to an almost uncritical reverence for St. Paul,
St. Augustine, Luther and their modern interpreters, especially Reinhold Niebuhr. I had come to the Seminary as
an idealistic and embryonic social reformer who sought in

the Church a platform and a base of operations; I left the Seminary a deeply convinced Christian churchman who was sure that only in the authentic Christian experience of judgment, forgiveness and the redeemed life of the Christian community was the real key to understanding and reforming society to be discovered.

A ministry of nineteen years has only served to reinforce my conviction about the adequacy and relevance of the Christian faith and my feeling that it has been most adequately and powerfully mediated to men through the balance of sacramental worship, Christian education, private prayer and corporate life which the Episcopal Church represents. I have seen the Episcopal Church and its work in a wide variety of situations. My ministry began in three small missions, located in the industrial suburbs of Los Angeles. The congregations were made up originally of people with English background, who found in the Episcopal Church the familiar ways of the Church of their childhood. We also began to reach out, however, to the large numbers of younger industrial workers and their families who were moving into the area. Our congregations, although relatively small in numbers, represented a wide cross-section of the communities in which they were located. School teachers, local business and professional people, industrial workers, retired elderly people—many of them English in origin—this was the kind of congregation to which I had to speak and minister. It was quite obvious that in these communities at any rate the Episcopal Church was anything but a "class church." It plainly had a wide and broad appeal, and we enjoyed gratifying growth, although beset by the usual difficulties of a small congregation.

After three years I was awarded the W. Cosby Bell Fellowship from the Virginia Seminary, and went to Yale Divinity School to pursue graduate studies in Church History. Here I was brought into contact with St. Paul's Church, New Haven, Connecticut. This fine old parish had had a great tradition of distinguished clerical leadership, and included among its members some of the fine old families of the city, several members of the Yale faculty, and an impressive number of rather simple and in some cases underprivileged people who lived in the neighborhood of the church. Once again the criticism of a "class church" seemed singularly inappropriate.

After two years in New Haven, which included the experience of teaching on the staff of the Berkeley Divinity School, I was called to be the rector of the Church of St. Matthew, San Mateo, California. On the surface, at least, the Church of St. Matthew might seem to justify the criticism that it was ministering predominantly to one class in society. The reason was that the community itself represented a generally high level of economic well-being. The peninsula area just south of San Francisco had been chosen by some of the early California millionaires as an ideal place to live. Around these old great estates had developed charming residential communities, catering very largely to people of substantial means. On the other hand, the parish included a very large number of less affluent people, living near the business center of the community. At the communion rail on a Sunday morning one might find kneeling side by side the president of one of San Francisco's leading banks or a leading society woman, and the Negro laundress at the hospital or the clerk at the local postoffice. Five years of wonderfully harmonious parish life convinced me that one of the few places where all elements of a community can find real fellowship and unity of purpose is in the worship of God and in His service.

From this lovely and highly privileged northern California suburb I went to be Dean of St. Paul's Cathedral, Los Angeles. Located in the downtown district, the Cathedral was suffering the fate often visited upon downtown churches. Its supporters were moving farther and farther out into the rapidly burgeoning suburbs of the great metropolis. The ambitious highway program of the city and state was destroying large numbers of apartment houses and small homes within the immediate vicinity of the Cathedral and the housing that remained was often of an undesirable sort. An inadequate transportation system made it difficult for people at a distance to come with any frequency to the services and activities. Without any significant endowment income, the Cathedral was obliged to support itself entirely from the gifts of its congregation, made up of an unusually high percentage of elderly people living on small pensions and annuities. All the personal, financial, moral—and psychiatric—problems of a great city flowed in and out of the Cathedral doors. The Dean of the Cathedral was also expected to take a very large part in the field of community leadership and in the direction of diocesan affairs.

As president of the Church Federation of Los Angeles for a year and a half, I was obliged to think not only of my own Cathedral congregation but of the wider religious

needs and opportunities of the whole community, as well
as of its social and moral character. As one of the leading
churches of the downtown area the Cathedral was looked to
to set a standard of liturgical dignity, musical excellence
and pulpit oratory for the whole diocese and community.
With meagre resources but with the sustaining enthusiasm of a remarkably generous congregation I spent four
and a half years in what I still consider one of the most
challenging situations anywhere in the Episcopal Church.

Columbia University needed a Chaplain. Traditionally
Anglican in its religious orientation, Columbia sought me
out as a possible candidate for the position. My friendship
with the former Chaplain, now Dean James A. Pike, had
already introduced me to some of the challenge and opportunity which the University Chaplaincy represented. I was
called, and accepted the position in 1952, assuming as well
the duties of Executive Officer of the Department of Religion. Here was a wholly new kind of ministry. No longer
was I the center of an admiring throng of parishioners,
drawn into a parish, in part at least, because they found
me and my ways of doing things congenial and attractive.
In the University I was only one of a vast machinery of
administrative and faculty personnel. Far from being the
acknowledged leader of the group in which I worked, the
very legitimacy and usefulness of my position was questioned by a large segment of the University community.
Neither I nor anybody else knew precisely what I was supposed to do! I was turned loose in one of the most stimulating and exciting academic centers of our American
society with the vague commission to represent the concerns and interest of religion. I was to add my small voice

—and a dubious addition it seemed to me—to the witness already being borne in New York City and more especially on Morningside Heights by some of the greatest ecclesiastical institutions of the whole nation. Not only could I no longer confine my own interests to those of the Episcopal Church, I was now asked to consider the needs of a community that was not even prepared to describe itself as Christian nor even as theistic.

What ministry and message does the Episcopal Church have in such a situation? I am still in the process of spelling out that answer. I am convinced, however, that only a Church which has a rich cultural heritage and background and which has had an experience of finding its place in the academic traditions throughout all of its history could be of much help to one in my position. The Church of Wycliffe, John Colet, Thomas Cranmer, Richard Hooker, John Donne, George Herbert, Samuel Johnson, William Wilberforce, John Henry Newman in his early years, Charles Kingsley, Frederick Denison Maurice, W. R. Inge, T. S. Eliot, and W. H. Auden, as well as a host of other philosophers, scientists, political thinkers, poets, novelists, and artists, will obviously know something about the kinds of questions which a university community is engaged in raising. So even now the Episcopal Church seems to me to be enormously relevant and significant in its potential role in the university scene.

This is the story of how I came to know the Episcopal Church and to find my place within its life and ministry. Our next business is to seek to express some of the great values and advantages that this tradition seems to me, as a result of my experiences, to possess.

TWO

"WHEN WE ASSEMBLE AND MEET TOGETHER"

FOR ME, as for many other newcomers to the Episcopal Church, the most important single impression it made was of the dignity and objectivity of its worship. My experiences with American Protestant worship had not, of course, been very wide. I had known a variety of Sunday schools and had found them rather boring as far as experiences of genuine worship were concerned. For the most part, the stress was on a study of the Bible, and what might be called worship was encompassed in a very brief and rather monotonous series of "opening exercises." Surely our Protestant programs of Christian education are seriously lacking at this point. When one realizes that for the greater part of its history the Christian Church has relied upon the experience of common worship to convey the meaning and significance of its faith, one becomes keenly aware of how impoverished any program of Christian training and nurture must inevitably be which lacks opportunities for introduction to and training in Christian worship. As the reader will realize from the first chapter of this little book, if a certain Lutheran Sunday School had paid somewhat less attention to Luther's *Short Catechism* and a little more to the authentic Lutheran liturgical genius, I might never have been an Episcopalian at all!

For the most part, however, even the adult congregation in most American Protestant churches participates in a life of worship which only very partially meets some of the criteria of an authentic Christian worship. In the first place, my experience with the worship of most Protestant churches has led me to the conviction that the element that might be identified as "objectivity" is sadly lacking. For the most part the congregation is the object of primary attention and their edification is thought of as the chief purpose of the church service. The traditional church architecture which is universally employed in Episcopal churches suggests at once to the person who comes into the church building that such is not the case here. At the center of the church building is the altar and the cross and the attention and respect paid to this area of the church building is symbolic of a genuine sense of the presence and reality of God in the midst of his people. As a choir boy I was, of course, instructed carefully about bowing reverently to the altar when I passed in front of it, keeping outside the altar rails unless some business directly connected with worship took me inside, facing toward the liturgical eastern end of the church where the altar was located to recite the Apostles' Creed, and in other ceremonial acts. No one made a great point about it but I was impressed forcibly with the fact that here was a kind

of Christianity that realized that God was the center of
Christian worship and that the presence of the congregation was only important in so far as it served to praise
and glorify Him.

Many years later I read a charming story by Cecil B.
de Mille in which he told of an occasion during his childhood when he went to a Lenten service in the nearby
Episcopal church, only to discover to his terror and surprise that he was the only member of the congregation!
Before he had time to flee, however, the rector had entered
the chancel and was beginning Evening Prayer. Mr. de
Mille records the deep impression that this clergyman's
conduct of the service made upon the little boy who constituted his entire congregation. The whole service was
read through carefully and reverently, just as if the church
were filled with worshippers. Mr. de Mille realized that
here was an attitude toward worship that regarded God
as the center of it all and whether there were two worshippers or two thousand was a matter of relative in-
difference.

Equally impressive was the assumption that worship was
an activity in which the congregation took an active part.
Gradually there dawned upon me the significance of the
fact that in the Episcopal church the place where the congregation sits is *not* called an "auditorium." The congregation is not there just to "audit"; they are there to
worship. There are important things for them to do.
They have parts of the service to say. They attest to their
meaningful participation in the service by standing, kneeling and sitting down at the appropriate places. It was a
great relief to a small boy—as it has continued to be a relief

to a mature man—to know that worship was something that one could participate in by saying certain things and doing certain things quite independent of special religious or spiritual feelings or sentiments. God is glorified by any conscientious and honest act of adoration even if the heart is lukewarm and the mind dulled with weariness. Since worship is something offered to God and not something primarily designed to induce religious experiences in the worshipper, an Episcopalian is mercifully relieved of the appalling responsibility that seems to rest upon members of some churches of the pietist tradition of perennially scrutinizing their religious consciousness and analyzing and evaluating their supposedly spiritual sentiments. It was not that such sentiments did not occasionally overcome me, and still do in surprising and unexpected moments in worship—but that such experiences were quite incidental to the main business of worship.

I found that what is true of any art is true also of worship—it creates its deepest effect when it is least concerned with effect, it has its greatest power when it is most completely dedicated to the purity and integrity of its art. To hear a group of boy choristers singing the Psalms in Westminster Abbey can transport me into the seventh heaven, but it does so precisely because the choristers are completely caught up in the task of rendering as purely and beautifully as they can the words and music of the text to the praise and glory of God. The rediscovery of the art of worship in Protestantism has been marred to some extent by a kind of self-conscious theatricalism which seems to have as its primary object creating what is rather barbarously called "a worship experience." It must be con-

fessed that in some Episcopal churches this same corrupt-
ing and degrading idea is also to be found. The real art
of worship will never come into its own until it loses its
self-consciousness and seeks as its chief object the pure and
unalloyed adoration and worship of Almighty God.

In order to secure the ends and results described above,
the Episcopal Church has always, of course, been dedicated to the principle of *liturgical* worship. While the
exact derivation of the word is somewhat uncertain, there
is evidence to suggest that the word "liturgy" derives from
two Greek words "laos," meaning "people" and "ergos,"
meaning "work." The liturgy is that which the people do
together. Since this is the case there must be prescribed
rules and agreed upon forms by which the service proceeds. Only in a service which the worshipper can depend
upon to move in a certain way and to take a certain form
will the worshipper be sufficiently at home to take a lively
and intelligent part. So-called "extemporaneous" prayer or
"free worship" inevitably produces a kind of hesitancy on
the part of the congregation because of the uncertainty as
to what is going to happen next.

It must be confessed that the result of the use of such
forms of worship, agreed upon and universally employed,
is sometimes a kind of empty formalism. This is perhaps all the more dangerous because of the magnificent
but oftentimes obscure sixteenth- and seventeenth-century
English in which most of the Prayer Book is written. It
would be an interesting experiment to enquire what meaning the average Episcopal layman gives to such phrases as:
"Grant that Thy grace may always prevent and follow us"
or "that after this life we may have the fruition of Thy

glorious Godhead." (In order not to leave the uninstructed reader in hopeless frustration, let me say that "prevent" has, of course, the old meaning of "go before" and that the word "fruition" means "enjoyment.") There is a kind of insidious narcotic quality about some of the Prayer Book language which almost invites the reader or the hearer into a kind of spiritual stupor. Unfortunately the art of translation is an exceedingly rare one, and modern attempts to rewrite the Prayer Book have not been conspicuously successful. To Archbishop Thomas Cranmer the Anglican communion owes a great deal but in no instance is that debt more conspicuous than in the leadership which he exercised in the translation of the Book of Common Prayer. The American Prayer Book, of course, is a modification of the English Prayer Book of 1662 (still the official liturgy of the Church of England). The most recent revision of the American Prayer Book was accomplished in 1928 and seems to continue to serve satisfactorily as the official medium for the Episcopal church's worship.

One of the chief advantages of liturgical worship lies in the insurance it gives of balance and proportion. Free worship and extemporaneous prayer rarely (except in the case of the few individual clergymen who are geniuses in the art of public worship) achieve the level of excellence in these respects that is everywhere evident in the services of the Book of Common Prayer. Each service has its own "rationale"—an orderly plan by which the service proceeds through a number of phases and expresses the whole range of Christian worship. The Order for Daily Morning Prayer, for example, begins with a reminder that the congregation is in the presence of God, and that it is His service and worship to which they are primarily to devote themselves. This is expressed in the opening sentences, including such magnificent scriptural passages as "The Lord is in his holy temple; let all the earth keep silence before him"; or "Thus saith the high and lofty One that inhabiteth eternity whose name is Holy; I dwell in the high and holy place, with him also that is of a contrite and humble spirit, to revive the spirit of the humble, and to revive the heart of the contrite ones." But to be in the presence of God is to be aware at once of one's own inadequacies, of the broken and deformed character of one's life and of the life of one's society, to be aware, to put it bluntly, of one's sins. So the opening sentences are followed by an invitation to a general confession in which the Christian mood of penitence is given striking expression. "We have erred and strayed from thy ways like lost sheep. We have followed too much the devices and desires of our own hearts. We have offended against thy holy laws. We have left undone those things which we ought to have done; and we have done those things which we ought not to have done; and there is no health in us."

A skeptical agnostic college professor said to me many years ago, "The General Confession of the Episcopal Book of Common Prayer is one part of the service that I can join in *ex animo!*" By couching the general confession in the language of the first person *plural,* the Church reminds us that many of our sins are social in character, that we are bidden to confess not just our personal peccadillos but the great injustices and failures of the family, the community, the church, the nation and the world of nations. What could be more salutary or strike a more responsive chord in most human hearts? Following the Confession come the calming and powerful words of Absolution: "He pardoneth and absolveth all those who truly repent, and unfeignedly believed his holy Gospel." Thus reassured of God's acceptance and forgiveness, the worshipper expresses his gratitude first of all in the great liturgical prayer of the Christian ages, the Lord's Prayer. Following this, the Order for Daily Morning Prayer prescribes an alternation of praise and instruction, using the Psalms and lessons from the Old and New Testaments. This is followed by the recitation of the Apostles' Creed, an ancient baptismal formula, intended to express in summary fashion the whole great story of God's mighty acts on behalf of His people and suitable therefore as a kind of summary of the great truths of which the Old and New Testament lessons have been partial statements. Then follow the Collects, or stated prayers, one for the particular day or season of the church year and the others, prayers for peace and for grace, for the President of the United States, for clergy and people, for "all conditions of men" and such other prayers as may seem suitable in the particular setting of the particular service. A General Thanksgiving is provided and often used at the end of the prayers of intercession, the whole service ending with the Grace. Very few services that any one individual might contrive could match the balance and sweep and sense of progress of this liturgical formulation. Those who have worshipped by means of such a service, far from feeling cramped and inhibited and restricted by it have found that it leads them deeper and deeper into the knowledge of God and of His ways with each repetition of its use.

Not only does each Prayer Book service proceed according to a carefully balanced plan of its own but through the use of the traditional Christian calendar the services during the year stress first one and then another of the main biblical themes in such a way as to bring the whole Christian story to the attention of the worshipper. In Advent the significance of Christ for the ultimate issues of human life and history is stressed; in the Christmas and the Epiphany seasons the reality and meaning of His coming into human life; in Lent the sharp challenge which Christ's life presents to the easy-going ways of the world, a challenge which becomes dramatically focussed in the events of Passiontide and Holy Week; in Good Friday and Easter the triumphant reassurance of God's ultimate victory even in the crises of suffering, failure and death; in Ascensiontide the ultimate authority of Christ and His kingdom over the whole creation; in Whitsuntide the ongoing work of Christ through the person of the Holy Spirit, especially within the life and fellowship of the Christian Church; and in the long Trinity season the meaning of this great Christian story for our whole attitude toward life and its problems and opportunities. So the Christian year is simply the way in which the Episcopal Church expresses its concern that the whole of the Bible in its main emphases shall engage the attention of the Christian worshipper throughout a twelve-month period. Rather than depending upon the range of interests of any given clergyman, influenced by the many pressures which crowd the calendar with days of civic or community concern, the Episcopal Church by its careful adherence to the traditional Christian calendar ensures for its worshippers the perennial exercise of hearing again the great Christian story in its fullness.

Formalism is the occupational disease of any Christian worshipper, no matter whether he be committed to the principle of extempore prayer or to liturgical prayer. Who has not known clergymen of the Free Church tradition who in their so-called "extemporaneous" prayers repeated hackneyed and meaningless phrases with a formalism that equalled or exceeded that of the most unimaginative advocate of liturgical worship. Part of my early ministry was spent in a community which was in those days a singularly drab and cheerless place, the dumping ground of unfortunate victims of the depression of the 30's, a place of substandard housing, organized gambling, and general dreariness. One of the local ministers, whenever called upon to lead in prayer at community or civic ceremonies, invariably began with the words "O God, we thank Thee for ———ville." It occurred to me many times that God had had all too little to do with the development of ———ville and that in any case He didn't deserve much credit for it! Surely here was formalism, and what is more a formalism based upon a rather barren and unimaginative literary pattern.

To lead liturgical worship does require constant vigilance. The very existence of a pattern and form of words can be a temptation to careless preparation and sloth. The results, of course, are inevitably disastrous. However, a conscientious clergyman or individual worshipper by a certain amount of thoughtful preparation and careful attention over a period of years to the familiar words which stand before him in the pages of the Prayer Book will find himself entering into the richest treasure house of Christian devotion and piety to be found anywhere in the English language outside the pages of the Bible itself. If I were to cite one single reason why I became and still remain an Episcopalian, I think I would point to the Book of Common Prayer and to its universal acceptance in the Anglican communion as the basis for Christian life and worship.

One of the dangers in the present revival of religion in America is that it will buy popularity by appealing only to the immediately felt needs of people. Biblical religion, on the contrary, has often told people that their felt needs are far from measuring the real depths of their problems. The Prayer Book has seemed to me more and more to be the best guarantee that the real dimensions of the human problem and the real clue to its resolution will continue to be set before the congregation of God's people Sunday after Sunday, week in and week out, in a balanced and orderly way. Whatever the minister may say or fail to say in his sermon, no congregation using the Book of Common Prayer will for long accept any easy solution of the problems of human existence nor any watered down estimate of the true goal of human life. The profundities of the General Confession, the Burial Office, the moving language by which the sacraments of Holy Baptism and the Holy Communion are celebrated and administered—all of this and much else besides in this great depository of Christian devotion and aspiration rebukes the easy amiability of a moralistic pulpit and the "get-spiritual-quick" ambition which often infects the pew. A liturgical life which initially attracted me by its dignity and beauty now appeals to me most deeply as a way of mediating to men the genuine depth and richness of the biblical view of life.

Theoretically this might be provided by a painstaking and thorough-going reading of the Bible undertaken by an individual on his own, but as a matter of practice for most church members this is hardly a live option. To worship by the Prayer Book—which in itself draws heavily upon Biblical material or upon paraphrasings of it—is to confront the biblical faith, epitomized and made concrete in terms of perennial Christian needs and concerns. The widespread use, for example, of the Book of Common Prayer even among churches of the "free worship" tradition on occasions such as burial and marriages indicates the success it has had in rendering the biblical faith in a convenient and usable way as the theme and motif of Christion worship and life. To be able to take for granted in the regular worshipping life of the church the magnificence of the Prayer Book has always seemed to me one of the great glories of the Episcopal Church.

THREE

"OUTWARD AND VISIBLE SIGNS OF . . . GRACE"

I HAVE tried to say in the last chapter that one of the attractions of the Episcopal Church for me was the element of objectivity in its worship. This objectivity is seen most clearly in the sacramental character of the life of an Episcopalian. In its broadest meaning, our whole world is sacramental. That is to say, every time I shake you by the hand, or salute the flag, or put on an academic cap and gown and hood, I am illustrating the prevalence of the principle that outward and visible actions and things serve to convey spiritual meanings. We shall see in the next chapter that the Episcopal Church makes maximum use of this principle, which is written into nature and the longest standing customs of human society. Color, architecture, gesture, music, vestments—all these things can be used for the greater glory of God.

The Prayer Book defines a sacrament, however, in a more precise way: "An outward and visible sign of an inward

44

and spiritual grace given unto us, ordained by Christ Himself as a means whereby we receive this grace and a pledge to assure us thereof." Two sacraments have a clear claim to primary attention on this definition, being plainly "ordained by Christ Himself" in the pages of the New Testament; these are Holy Baptism and the Holy Communion, or as the Prayer Book alternatively calls it, the Lord's Supper or the Eucharist. Apparently the Prayer Book prefers to avoid the mediaeval name of Mass. The name of the feast of the Nativity is "commonly called Christmas Day," but this is the only use of the name except in a derogatory sense in the whole book.

The Episcopal Church, following the usage of an overwhelming majority of present-day Christian churches and of the almost unanimous verdict of the Church down through the ages, practices infant baptism. Indeed the parents are urged "that they defer not the baptism of their children." Here again the objectivity of Anglican worship is demonstrated. God can work an all-important change in a person's life long before the person is aware of it. This seems such a plain fact in other areas of life that one wonders why it was ever questioned in the area of religion. A child is a member of his family from the day he opens his eyes. He will know nothing of the family's name or its standards or its ideals or its history for many years to come. This does not mean that from the very beginning he is not participating in a very real sense in that family's life and is not receiving from his membership in it all kinds of formative and determinative influences. He may later prove unworthy of the family. He may flaunt its finest traditions and renounce any responsibility for its life, but he can never deny that he belongs to that family and belonged to it from the day he was born. The Episcopal Church and other Churches which practice infant baptism take a similar view of Holy Baptism. It makes a child a member of Christ; it draws him into the environment of Christ's household and family, the Church; it initiates a process that, quite without the child's knowing it, will shape and form his life and his attitudes. Can anyone deny that this child is a member of the Church? The Episcopal Church at least dares not deny it, and believes it is following the Spirit of its Lord who rebuked the disciples when they sought to hinder children from coming to Him and assured them of a welcome place in His presence and company.

The Episcopal Church follows carefully the New Testament directions for the administration of Holy Baptism, using invariably water and the formula of the invocation of the Holy Trinity ("In the name of the Father and of the Son and of the Holy Ghost"). Indeed any baptism which is administered in this way is accepted as a valid baptism, no matter where or by whom performed. Following the ancient usage of the early Church, established when life was somewhat uncertain and the possibility of a baptized child coming inadvertently into the care of a pagan family was very real, the Episcopal Church makes use of the institution of God-parents, two God-mothers and a God-father being required for a girl baby, and two God-fathers and a God-mother being required for a boy baby. Since the duties of the God-parents are very important as a part of the presuppositions of the administration of the sacrament of Baptism, most Episcopal clergy require that the God-parents themselves be baptized persons and receive some instruction in their duties and responsibilities.

The Prayer Book makes no mention of the possibility—except in a grave emergency—of a Baptism being held anywhere but in the church building itself. The growing custom of holding Baptisms at a time when the majority of the congregation can be present has everything to commend it—excepting only the consequent anxiety of proud mothers lest the little candidate disgrace the family "before all those people"! Baptism is not some magical rite of mysterious significance; it has the plain and obvious—albeit incalculable—effect of initiating the child into the new environment of the Christian family of the Church. What is more natural than that the members of this wider family shall be present on such an auspicious occasion? Anxious mothers will do well to remember with what tolerance the antics of the very young and innocent are regarded, and accept whatever minor embarrassments are involved as the price of the thrilling sense of the great company of faithful people into which the newly baptized child is being brought. The Episcopal Church follows the ancient Church's custom of beginning the observance of the great Easter festival by the administration of Holy Baptism, usually late on the afternoon of Easter Even.

Baptism is the sacrament of Christian initiation; the Holy Communion is the sacrament of Christian sustenance and renewal. From the earliest times it has been regarded as the central act of worship in the Christian community. The *Apology* of Justin Martyr, for example, written in the middle of the second century, describes it as the characteristic way in which Christians express their faith and their devotion. Incidentally, Justin's description sounds remarkably like any celebration of the Holy Communion in an Episcopal parish, even to the use of the ancient formula "Lift up your hearts" and the response "We lift them up unto the Lord" as a prelude to the act of consecrating the bread and wine. The Holy Communion holds this central place in Christian life and worship because it so superbly sums up and expresses the deepest Christian convictions about God and human life. The Prayer Book service emphasizes first of all the incredible demand that God makes upon man summed up in the Ten Commandments or our Lord's more positive version of the Divine Law—"thou shalt love God with all thy heart . . . and soul . . . and mind and thy neighbor as thyself." Then in the Epistle and the Gospel this demand is matched by the offer that God has made to us of His Son, and the meaning of this offer is defined more clearly in the ancient creed of Nicea, which insists that it was not only that God *sent* Christ but that God *came* in Christ and shared in the lot and destiny of mankind. This is more precisely and particularly expounded in the sermon which follows.

Then, even as it was in the second century, the offering follows—not just an embarrassing necessity if the utilities are to be paid and the minister's salary kept up—but an expression of the fact that God welcomes man's gifts of himself, of his labor, of his capacity and strength. In Justin's day there was very little money in circulation—especially among poorer people like the Christians—and so the offering was often bread and wine, gifts in kind, as we should say. Today in many Episcopal churches this ancient symbolism is maintained as men and women bring up from the congregation at the offering time not only the gifts of money but also the very bread and wine which are to be used in the Holy Communion. The bread and the wine are symbols of the gifts of God's creation, moulded and shaped and made usable by the talent and skill and intelligence of man. To these offerings are added the prayers and intercessions of the congregation, and then— as if to say, "But neither our offerings nor our prayers are good enough for God"—the congregation makes its most important offering of all, the sacrifice of a broken and a contrite heart, in the General Confession.

After the assurance of pardon and forgiveness, which means that God accepts our offerings tainted and unworthy though they are, we are ready to bless and consecrate them and make them the means by which God's love and power can enter more fully into our lives. Like ancient Judaism, the Church blesses by giving thanks, by ascribing to God the glory and the virtue of life. "Let us give thanks," says the priest, again using the language of St. Justin's description, and the people respond: "It is meet and right so to do." Then in the solemn prayer of consecration the priest recalls to us the offering that God made in Christ, an offering that covers the inadequacies of our offerings, and which takes our offerings and gives them back to us in the act of communion, with the assurance that we are receiving now the very substance of our Lord's life into our lives. "The Body of our Lord Jesus Christ, which was given for thee, preserve thy body and soul unto everlasting life. Take and eat this in remembrance that Christ died for thee and feed on Him in thy heart by faith with thanksgiving." After a

brief prayer of thanksgiving and the blessing, the service
is over.

What could more eloquently portray the deepest realities
of the Christian life—God's demands, God's offer, our
offerings, our sin, God's forgiveness, new power to live in
Him, with Him in us? The Episcopal Church is content
that men shall find these realities in her service of the
Holy Communion, and does not press precise definitions
as to just what happens or how it happens. There is no
definition of the doctrine of Christ's presence in the Holy
Communion, although in the Articles of Religion the
definition of Transubstantiation is rejected as inconsistent
with the Church's understanding of a sacrament. (Apparently the compilers of the Articles believed that the view
that when God makes use of material things He must
destroy their inner reality is really to "overthrow the
nature of a sacrament" and to deny the essential compati-
bility between nature and spirit which the whole sacramental principle is intended to express and defend.) It is
abundantly clear that the Prayer Book believes that Christ
is present in the Holy Communion—although it will not
define just how or just when or just where. Episcopalians
differ on these matters and have differed for hundreds of
years.

What is more important is that the Holy Communion
continues to be the center of the Church's worshipping life;
it is the natural expression in high festival moments like
Christmas and Easter or in other moments of corporate or
personal significance—at the consecration of a bishop or the
ordination of a deacon or a priest, at a marriage or a
funeral, in times of sickness and distress—of the Chris-

tion faith in Christ and His power to heal and forgive and save. No words can describe what an Episcopalian finds Sunday after Sunday, day after day, year in and year out, as he brings to the altar rail his problems, his joys, his successes, his failures, his sins, his victories over temptation and despair. The Prayer Book itself tries to sum it up in the prayer of thanksgiving after the Communion has been finished: "We most heartily thank thee, for that thou dost vouchsafe to feed us . . . with the spiritual food of the . . . Body and Blood of thy Son . . . and dost assure us thereby of thy favour and goodness towards us; and that we are very members incorporate in the mystical body of thy Son, which is the blessed company of all faithful people; and are also heirs through hope of thy everlasting kingdom." Our status as God's children, our status as brethren one of another; our status as heirs of the promises of a fulfillment which will exceed all that we can desire— all this is reaffirmed every time we come to be fed with Christ's own life. This is the heart and center of the Christian life, and every Episcopalian is grateful for the long tradition which magnifies its importance and multiplies the opportunities for its celebration.

"How many sacraments hath Christ ordained in His Church?" asks the Offices of Instruction. The answer is somewhat ambiguous: "Two only as generally necessary to salvation." It may be objected that this does not fully answer the question. Some Episcopalians, following the rather arbitrary numbering of Peter Lombard in the Middle Ages, say there are seven: Confirmation, Holy Matrimony, Unction of the sick and dying, Holy Orders, Penance, in addition, of course, to Baptism and the Holy

Communion. This venerable reckoning has the advantage of corresponding to the great crises and needs of human life—birth (Baptism); adolescence (Confirmation); marriage (Holy Matrimony); authorized leadership (Holy Orders); cleansing (Penance); sustenance (Holy Communion); sickness and death (Unction). Whether they are to be reckoned strictly as sacraments, the truth is that all of them are used in the Episcopal Church.*

Confirmation takes place when the child who has, as we have already tried to show, ever since his baptism been in truth and reality a member of the Church, takes upon himself the personal obligations and responsibilities of that membership. The Christian experience of God's grace and power is that it is poured out discriminatingly and appropriately. A man who takes on the mature and responsible relationship of a confirmed member of the Church obviously has need of God's power and God's guidance in ways which other men could know nothing of at all. So two things happen at a Confirmation—a person "confirms" the vows of his baptism and assumes them for himself; the bishop lays his hands upon his head and calls down the power and assistance of the Holy Spirit that he may "be confirmed" in this resolution and fulfil it "more and more until he come unto thy everlasting kingdom." The Episcopal Church administers Confirmation only by the Bishop presumably in order that it may be clear that the candidate is being admitted in full responsible membership not into one single parish but into a world-wide and age-old Christian fellowship. The Bishop makes a visitation—usually at

---

* Because the Episcopal Church's views on the ministry are set forth elsewhere, Holy Orders is not discussed in this chapter.

least once a year—to confirm the candidates, to renew his associations with the parish, its people and clergy, and to remind them once again of their wider obligations and relationships. His authority over them is—as we shall see— primarily pastoral and fatherly; and his coming is a high point in the year's experiences.

Whether marriage is to be counted as a sacrament may be doubted on the grounds that it was not "instituted of Christ," but that it is sacramental in its character, that it employs a physical relationship to teach deep meanings of mutuality and love and even to symbolize the care and concern which Christ has for the Church is undeniably the teaching of the Bible and of 2000 years of Christian tradition. Because the Episcopal Church holds this high estimation of the marriage state, it believes that marriage must be life-long. To grow together in mutual understanding and self-giving requires a lifetime of disciplined care and thoughtfulness which rests not upon the varying tides of emotion but upon a steady determination of the whole heart and mind and will. Our sentimental and romantic views of love—largely dependent upon Hollywood where love is what happens to Clark Gable when he first catches sight of Lana Turner—are flatly contradicted by the marriage service of the Prayer Book, which requires a man to *promise* "to love and to cherish till death us do part." Love is a matter of decision, of promise, of determination— not only a matter of emotion and feeling and impulse. A man is drawn to a woman by these things; in marriage he promises to transform this initial attraction into a union and mutuality described by our Lord as being made "one flesh."

Unhappily not all the relationships which are called
marriages begin with this determination, and of those that
do, many come to grief against the hard and stubborn facts
of human self-assertiveness and pride and wilfulness. Our
Lord once admitted that because of "the hardness of men's
hearts" the ideal of marriage is sometimes frustrated. What
shall the Church do in such cases? They are the trial of
every conscientious Episcopal clergyman. He will feel deep
sympathy with a couple, one or both of whom for one reason
or another have terminated legally their marriage to another
partner and now desire to start again and rescue the experience of married love in another relationship. Indeed
in some cases the clergyman will even have counseled a
divorce and will advise the desirability of another marriage.
What can the Church do? It cannot lightly allow its service
to be repeated again, for what meaning could then be
given to the solemn words "until death us do part"? In
some cases, it may be determined that some disabling
circumstance justifies the Bishop's decision that in the eyes
of the Church no valid marriage took place in the first
instance and that the couple are therefore free to marry
as if they were being married for the first time—as indeed
they are in the eyes of the ecclesiastical authorities. Sometimes this course of action is not possible. The Episcopal
Church must then decline to solemnize the marriage, but
it does not exclude those who enter into such a marriage—
outside the Church obviously—from the benefits of the
Church's life and worship. On presentation to the Bishop
of evidence that the parties desire to establish a true Christian marriage, he may re-affirm their communicant status
in the Church's fellowship. This seems to some to be

legalistic and picayune. To others it seems a wise, if somewhat illogical, combination of two things—a strong witness to the world of the Church's ideal of marriage as a lifelong union of man and woman and a pastoral sympathy for those who because of "the hardness of men's hearts" have not been able to fulfil one of the conditions of that ideal. This will satisfy neither the rigorist who would exclude such people from communion and Church fellowship forever afterward nor the liberal who would re-marry them again without heeding the consequences of such a use of the Church's marriage service. As in so many things the Episcopal Church has found itself in a "middle way"— logically difficult to defend and maintain but found in experience to correspond to the anomalies and paradoxes of life itself.

Even more important than the Church's way of dealing with marriage failures is the Church's way of seeking to avoid such failures as far as possible. The parish priest must give instruction on the nature of Christian marriage as one of his chief responsibilities. Any couple seeking to be married must receive such instruction and must notify the priest three days at least before the proposed ceremony so that he may arrange such preparation. In cases of marital discord, the Canon Law requires the couple to report the discord to the minister if it threatens to destroy the marriage so that the minister may labor for a reconciliation. Many couples have testified that in the difficulties of their marriage—and what marriage does not have some such rocks and pitfalls—nothing was more helpful than the experience of going together to the Holy Communion, confessing together their failures and shortcomings, hearing the assurance of absolution, and receiving the Body and Blood of the loving and self-giving Christ in pardon and in renewal of life. This is one of the reasons why the Church requires that at least one of the parties to any proposed marriage must be a baptized person, and that the couple intend to take seriously their religious obligations and to make worship and prayer a part of their lives as a couple and a family.

Penance came to be associated in the mediaeval Church with the practice of auricular confession to the priest. Aware of the dangers of this system as a general require- ment—dangers of pettiness and over-scrupulosity—the An- glican Reformation did away with the requirement and for the average person under average circumstances prescribed instead a "General Confession" to be said together with the rest of the congregation and a general absolution to be said by the priest to the people "being penitent." This assumed that most people most of the time know something of the meaning of the power of sin in their own lives—or can be assisted to that knowledge by sermons, Bible reading, self- examination,—and are able to acknowledge that sin in their hearts and to seek God's forgiveness. More than four hundred years of Anglicanism proves that assumption to be sound.

There is, however, always the possibility of exceptions, of people who are perplexed in conscience, who need not just general exhortation, general confession and general absolution but a more particular treatment of a special problem. Episcopalians differ as to their belief about the frequency with which such instances occur. Some Anglo- Catholic priests and parishes assume that they occur fairly frequently and urge their people to make use on a regular basis of an adaptation of the traditional form of the Sacrament of Penance. The great majority of Episcopalians, on the other hand, find such instances rare. Of course, every Episcopal priest is prepared to hear a private confession. This obligation is implied in the words of the Exhortation at the end of the Communion service: "if there be any of you, who by this means (i.e., general confession after personal self-examination) cannot quiet his own conscience herein, but requireth further comfort or counsel, let him come to me, or to some other Minister of God's Word, and open his grief, that he may receive such godly counsel and advice, as may tend to the quieting of his conscience, and the removing of all scruple and doubtfulness." No Episcopal priest is at liberty to require such a private confession as a prerequisite for admission to the Holy Communion. This arrangement seems to me to be another instance of the extraordinary wisdom and understanding of human nature—both of its weaknesses and of its possibilities—which at so many points marks the Anglican Communion and the Episcopal Church.

The mediaeval practice of Unction came to be reserved for cases in which death was regarded as imminent. As such, it was eliminated at the Reformation and only recently and with a new meaning—or perhaps we should say a recovery of its New Testament meaning and its usage in the primitive Church—has it once again found its way into the Prayer Book. It is now regarded as a legitimate part of the Church's ministry to the sick and far from being reserved for use in cases where death is imminent expresses in its present form the purpose of healing and restoration.

"When a sick person," says the Prayer Book, "shall in humble faith desire the ministry of *healing* through Anointing or the Laying on of Hands, the Minister may, etc." (Italics mine) The prayers that follow refer to "soundness of health" and ask that "all thy pain and sickness of body being put to flight, the blessing of health may be restored unto thee."

It was perhaps inevitable that as a Church committed to the sacramental principle the Episcopal Church should be one of the leaders in the revival among the traditional churches of the ministry of healing. Psychosomatic analysis of disease should come as no surprise to an Episcopalian, for he has testified to the reality of man as a psychosomatic being every time he has participated in any of the Church's sacraments. Of course, one's mind and body and spirit are all intimately related, and the disorders of one aspect of his personality are reflected in the whole personality. In this sense, a bodily healing may be regarded—as the New Testament regards it in many instances—as a sign of the coming of the Kingdom of God, as a sign that faith and self-forgetfulness have put to flight the power of fear and anxiety and self-assertiveness. What is not justified, of course, is any view that sickness is always curable provided only that enough faith be brought to bear on the situation. Death is abolished only at the Resurrection of the dead . . . "the last enemy that shall be destroyed is death." Mysterious as it may be, death is a universal experience for all of us, and sickness and infirmity is a reminder of that inescapable destiny. Fortunately, any healing movement in the Episcopal Church is set in the context of the Prayer Book in its totality, which helps to insure (but admittedly does

not entirely insure) against faddist and one-sided misunderstandings of the real Christian attitude toward disease and
death. I confess that I have had a devout Episcopalian tell
me with great pride that she had never allowed herself to
be examined by a physician and that she never would,
because she believed that God could heal her. I wondered
why on the same theory she bothered to eat or go to a
dentist, but the pressures of time made a coward of me and
I kept my wonderings to myself. A sacramental view of
life will accept all that the physician can discover and can
prescribe as a means of achieving health and vigor for the
tasks of life. Surely the greatest ministry of healing the
Episcopal Church performs is through the services of her
doctors and nurses and in her Church-operated hospitals
and convalescent homes. That God can and does work also
through the ministrations of a priest, who by assuring a
man of the forgiveness of his sins and of a new status as
God's child can release new impulses in him for health and
soundness, is the basis for the Church's ministry of spiritual
healing. Every priest can testify to the wonders it has
wrought.

Although it is not a sacrament, the Episcopal Church's
ministry at the time of death is one of its great glories and
deserves a word of explanation. A college professor told me
recently that although he never came to the Chapel it was
a comfort to know that when he died he would have such
a dignified and straightforward and moving burial service.
Perhaps the Episcopal Church has over-sold itself! The
majestic and yet simple atmosphere of the Burial service
is one way in which many people know the Episcopal
Church who know it in no other way. Perhaps it will in

time lead some of them to inquire further about a Church
that treats the solemn fact of death with such restraint,
such profundity, and such realism. There is no conspiracy
to hide the facts. Death has reached into the human community and left a gaping hole in its fabric. That fact is
faced in all seriousness and solemnity. It is not just that
someone has "gone through a door" or "passed away"
(whatever that means) or "gone away for a while." "The
Lord gave and the Lord hath taken away" is the simple and
stark fact as the Prayer Book sees it. In the committal the
Minister is directed to say: "Earth to earth, ashes to ashes,
dust to dust." It is curious in an age which has made so
much of realism that this honesty should be almost too
much to face, and that many people should gladly welcome the attempts of some funeral directors and cemeteries
(significantly re-named "Memorial Parks") to gloss over
the realities. The fact of death, however, is faced under the
perspective of God's fatherly care, our Lord's death and
resurrection, the conviction that individuals have an eternal significance precisely in their individuality as that individuality finds expression in trust and in love. There is
therefore no wracking rehearsal of the virtues of the deceased, a fact that insures the essential democracy of the
service. How false many eulogies must seem in God's eyes . . .
some of them obviously saying too much, some of them obviously saying too little. Only God who knows the secrets of
the heart can deliver an adequate eulogy, and so the Episcopal service is content to remind us that He cares, that in
Christ He forgives, that He receives and fulfils beyond our
comprehension or understanding. When it has said that and
prayed for that blessing upon the deceased and upon those

who mourn and upon us all who are made aware once again of the vanity of life apart from the Christian faith—then the Church is content to carry the body to its resting place and commit it "in sure and certain hope of the Resurrection unto eternal life," and the service is concluded.

I cannot imagine my Christian life apart from the sacramental life of the Episcopal Church, its ability to uncover in all the great experiences of life something of God's grace and God's purpose and God's power, its use of the things of sense—water, bread and wine, the human hand—to convey the reality of that which is unseen but by which men live out their existence and set their course. The sacraments, as St. Irenaeus said in the second century, "proclaim harmoniously the unity of flesh and spirit." What an incalculable effect that idea has had in western culture and civilization! Because it has made God real to me as the ground and source and meaning of every aspect of existence, I am forever grateful for the sacramental life of the Episcopal Church.

FOUR

"IN THE BEAUTY OF HOLINESS"

THE first Episcopal church I ever stepped into would not be rated by any competent architect as an outstanding example of ecclesiastical art and architecture. It was a modest little frame building, without any stained glass windows, with a very much overcrowded chancel and sanctuary. And yet this modest building was the setting for my first real experience of a service of Christian worship which attempted to enlist every human art for the greater glory of God. An air of mystery and reverence permeated it. It was obviously not a building in which one engaged in idle conversation nor indeed in which the interests or ordinary ways of men were central. Attention focussed upon the altar and the cross which stood in the midst of it. During large parts of the service the minister, and sometimes the choir, actually turned their backs on the congregation, a dramatic symbol of the fact that in this building attention was focussed somewhere outside of human life

62

as it is ordinarily lived. A friend of mine once told me that perhaps more than any other single thing that could be named as responsible for drawing him to the Episcopal Church was the initial impression he had received of the objective reality of God in worship when the choir turned toward the altar to say the Apostles' Creed, although no minister was standing at the altar at the time. Obviously God and not man was the center of attention here, and to His worship and adoration every talent and gift of the human race were summoned and devoted.

I did not know, of course, the long historical background of this atmosphere and attitude. Only in my later studies did the story unfold of how Anglicanism determinedly held on to the rich tradition of the use of the human arts in worship against the zeal of Puritan reformers. The Puritans, of course, had much logic on their side. They insisted that since the Reformation represented a drastic overhauling of the medieval theology and a return to the original religion of the New Testament, so the outward life of the Church ought to symbolize this sharp discontinuity by a ruthless exclusion of anything reminiscent of the ways of worship in the past. With virtual unanimity the bishops of the Elizabethan Church shared this point of view. Richard Cox, made Bishop of Ely by Elizabeth I, wrote, for example, to one of his friends on the continent, "we are . . . constrained to our great distress of mind, to tolerate in our churches the image of the Cross and Him who was crucified: the Lord must be entreated that this stumbling block may at length be removed." Cox was referring to Elizabeth's insistence that the crucifix be retained in the churches, and although the unanimous opposition of the bishops per-

suaded her to withdraw from this position, she was not so
easily moved on other similar issues. One of the Royal In-
junctions of 1559 provided that the clergy were to be ap-
pareled as in the last year of Edward VI.

The bishops were greatly disturbed at this provision, for,
as one of them wrote, "we are not ignorant what occasion
the Papists will take from thence, as a cause of stumbling
to the weak . . . Retaining the outward habits and inward
feeling of popery, so fascinates the ears and eyes of the
multitude, that they are unable to believe, but that either
the Popish doctrine is still retained or at least that it will
shortly be restored." On this matter, however, the Queen
was adamant. Her reasons were presumably practical; she
sought to establish customs of church life which would
reassure the average man that the Church of England was
the same Church that his father and grandfather had
known and that Reformation did not mean an absolute
break with the past. Such temporizing struck the Puritan-
minded clergy as unworthy and dangerous. Although their
protests continued, and actually forced some slight modification of the enforcement of the royal injunction, Elizabeth
won the day.

The whole discussion, although it centered on a relatively minor point of the use of certain kinds of vestments,
was nevertheless symbolic of a determination of Anglicanism which has continued to the present day. If one wants
to measure the difference between the way in which Anglicanism retained its continuity with its past and the way
in which Puritanism radically destroyed that continuity,
let him consider the contrast between Westminster Abbey
in London and another great church dedicated to St. Peter,

the Cathedral in Geneva. In the Abbey in London the past is gratefully accepted and helps to mold and fashion contemporary Christian life and worship. The altar, richly hung and ornamented, occupies its traditional place in the east end of the chancel. Rich wood carving ornaments the choir stalls, candles gleam, and choir and clergy are vested in ways that carry the imagination back for a thousand years. St. Peter's Cathedral in Geneva, while it has its own peculiar dignity, bears a very different aspect. Where the altar once stood, rows of unornamented benches provide space for an unvested choir. Although a plain table stands in front of this choir section, the obvious focus of attention is a large pulpit which stands on the left, well down into the nave of the Cathedral. No candles, rich embroidery, or ornamental woodwork soften the austerities of this building's interior, although some stained glass has made its appearance in the windows. No one will suggest that this setting for worship is without its own power and dignity, but it is bare and cold beside the warmth and richness of Westminster Abbey. In seeing these two churches I learned as I had never known before the meaning of the Anglican tradition.

The full richness of Anglican worship, of course, is not to be found in every village and hamlet. There are fearful and wonderful examples of poor taste in many Episcopal churches that one could mention, but the overall impression that one gains as he goes about the country is that again and again the Episcopal Church in a community, simple and modest as may be its proportions and adornment, breathes an atmosphere of God-centered worship that is suggested by few other Protestant churches in its neighborhood. Except for a few of the Colonial churches which were designed under the influence of the Evangelical Movement with its emphasis upon preaching and hence feature a great pulpit as the center of the building, most Episcopal churches focus the attention of the visitor at once upon the altar, the scene of the Sacrament of the Holy Communion which has become more and more the center and norm of the Church's worship. On most altars a cross is to be found, reminiscent of St. Paul's determination that Christ and Him Crucified must be the center of any genuine Christian faith and life. Usually candles also stand upon the altar, carrying the worshipper in imagination back to times when this was the only source of illumination. Time and tradition, however, have invested these candles with symbolic significance, two candles being representative of the divine and the human natures of our Lord, seven-branch candelabra reminding us of the ancient Hebrew number which symbolized the perfection of heaven, but perhaps the most eloquent suggestion of the symbolism of candles is that mentioned in the Royal Injunction of 1547, that two lights only should be placed upon the altar "to signify the joy and splendor we receive from the light of Christ's blessed Gospel." *

Centuries-old tradition govern the ornamentation of the altar. Although infrequently used in America, the English tradition calls for a richly ornamented "frontal," which covers the full length and height of the altar, oftentimes in the appropriate color for the season of the Church year and ornamented by embroidered symbols. More frequent in

* Quoted in Percy Dearmer's *"The Parson's Handbook,"* 1899, Milwaukee, the Young Churchman Company, page 20, *fn.*

American Episcopal churches is what is called the "super-frontal," a covering which hangs down for about a foot over the front of the altar, and also bears symbolic embroidery against the background of the seasonal color. A fair linen cloth covers the top of the altar and hangs down generously on both sides; this cloth bears five embroidered crosses, symbolizing the five wounds in the Body of the Crucified Christ. Forming the background for the altar, there will be perhaps a carved wood or stone reredos or a curtain, called a "dossal," either a permanent hanging or one which represents the seasonal colors and is changed correspondingly. Sometimes at right angles from the back wall stand two rods from which hang curtains which enclose the altar on either side. These are called "riddels." The altar, thus surrounded on three sides by curtains, is reminiscent of the Temple altar of Judaism, which was, however, completely surrounded by hangings to hide it from the eyes of the worshippers. The altar area, called the sanctuary, is generally divided from the rest of the chancel by rails, and custom prohibits unauthorized persons who have no part in the service at the altar from entering within these rails.

Most traditional Episcopal architecture calls for the choir to be placed between the sanctuary and the nave where the congregation sits. This follows, of course, the traditional cathedral style architecture, and in this area are placed the pulpit, the lectern from which lessons from the Bible are read, a reading desk for the clergyman to use in officiating at the so-called "choir offices" of Morning and Evening Prayer. So that the choir and ministers will not have to turn their backs either to the altar or to the congregation, the choir stalls are usually arranged at right

angles to the wall against which the altar stands. Both
pulpit and lectern are placed to one side so that for the
majority of the congregation sitting in the nave the view
of the altar is not interfered with. The font, in which baptisms are performed, is usually placed near the door of the
church, symbolizing the fact that it is by Baptism that
entrance and admission into the church takes place. Oftentimes, the church is designed in a cruciform manner, the
arms of the design being supplied by transepts, the head
of the cross design being the choir and sanctuary, and the
long vertical line being supplied by the nave. Although
this traditional pattern is found in an overwhelming number of Episcopal churches, architectural experimentation
has also found a ready response from Episcopal congregations. New interest in the liturgy and in public worship as
an expression of the essential social philosophy of the
Christian faith has resulted in daring new designs which
place the altar in the centre of the building so that the
majority of the congregation may have the most direct
view of it and access to it. A Joint Commission of the General Convention on Church Architecture and the Allied
Arts seeks to encourage creative originality both in church
design and in the ornamentation of church buildings and
the vestments of the clergy. Whatever new experiments
are made, however, they will reflect the long Anglican tradition which regards all the arts of mankind as useful aids
to worship and as legitimate offerings to the glory of God.

Clerical vestments, once one of the thorny problems of
Elizabethan Anglicanism, are now universally accepted
and valued in the Episcopal Church, both as a way of
symbolizing the distinctive ministry of the clergy in preach-

ing and worship and as testifying to the long history of
Christian devotion, reaching back nearly 2000 years. The
vestments which are used in many Episcopal churches, for
example, at the celebration of the Holy Communion, are
directly reminiscent of the customary dress of the Roman
citizen of 150 A.D. The customary vestments for the choir
offices do not have as long a history, but the academic
hoods and tippets may remind the worshipper of the age-
old alliance between religion and learning and conjure up
visions of monastic worship where a hood and a fur-lined
tippet were a necessity in a drafty and unheated medieval
chapel.

The retention of these traditional vestments is sometimes criticized for the reason that they suggest a sharp
separation between clergy and laity and also because they
seem to make Christianity so much a thing of the past. Is
there not a certain unreality about "dressing up" to look
like Roman citizens of the second century A.D. and does
it not make the clergy seem sharply separated and quite
remote from the workaday world of the laity? These ob-
jections, of course, have some weight, but they might
equally be pressed against the custom of academic dress at
solemn functions of the modern college or university. Although religion does have contemporary relevance if it is
to be treated seriously at all, Christianity as well as Judaism
is an historical faith. It looks to the past; it calls to remembrance what God has done in history. It insists that
the Holy Spirit has taught and led men through the experiences of two thousand years into much wisdom and insight.
The Christian religion is not something that the modern
worshipper is free to render as he likes. Although in one

important sense, each worshipper must make the Christian
faith his own, in another sense it is not his own at all but
is an historic faith, maintained at great cost, wise and rich
with the accumulated experience of the centuries, claim-
ing our attention today precisely because it has interpreted
and clarified life through such a long past. To go into an
Episcopal church and to take part in an Episcopal service
of worship makes all this eloquently apparent. The modern worshipper sees himself at once in proper perspective.
Here is something, obviously, that has been going on for
a long time before I arrived on the scene and presumably
will continue for a long time after I have left it. It is
something to which I, of course, may make a fresh and
creative contribution, but it is first of all something which
the labors and witness of others have handed on to me. My
first obligation is to understand it in all its historical richness, and then I shall perhaps be enabled to add something
of my own to this incredibly rich deposit. Someone has
said that the trouble with much modern Christianity is
that it has "failed to read the minutes of the previous meetings." By the outward aspect of its worship, the Episcopal
Church does much to correct this oversight.

The worship in an Episcopal Church is not only rich in
historical reminiscence; it is also surprisingly wise in its
psychological insights. The outsider will complain that to
worship as an Episcopalian is an extraordinarily strenu-
ous undertaking! Kneeling, sitting down, getting up, bowing—all of this, as well as continually trying to find one's
way through a prayer book—is a surprising way to worship
for one who is accustomed to sitting in a pew and simply
listening to what's going on. The Episcopal Church, how-

ever, is making use in these traditional postures of worship of a psychological insight which is ages old in its use but only recently has had experimental verification. The emotion, says psychology, often follows the action. It is not only true that one runs away because he is afraid; it is also true that the act of running away augments the fear. The proposal of the heroine in the Rodgers and Hammerstein musical comedy, *The King and I,* that suggests the strategy of "whistling a happy tune" whenever one is afraid, is a sound psychological device. The Episcopal Church is aware that human emotion is a very undependable thing indeed. One's moods are often sluggish and earthbound and stubornly resistant to the soaring and lifting themes of Christian adoration and worship. It helps, however, to *do* something to express this mood which the Church would instill. Just the simple act of kneeling when one comes into a church, a custom which is followed by all Episcopalians, will help to turn the thoughts and mood of the worshipper toward God and to lift him above the level of his own immediate anxieties and ambitions. To sit down to listen to a Lesson from the Bible and then to stand to join in a great hymn of adoration such as the Te Deum does not necessarily mean, of course, that one will be attentive to the Lesson nor that his spirit will rise automatically in ecstatic praise and adoration to match the ancient hymn of praise. The posture and the gesture, however, do help to create the mood and the attitude. What is more, of course, the very experience of watching others actively participating in worship in these ways helps to overcome one's own sluggishness and to quicken his sensi-

tivity to the reality of God and the way in which He touches
and helps human life.

Some newcomers are baffled by the seeming variety,
however, of these ceremonial usages which they find practiced both by the clergy and the congregation. They feel
that as newcomers they will be conspicuous by their failure
to do what others are doing at the right place and in the
right way. It will help to reassure such people to remind
them that many Episcopalians are as baffled as they are
by some things they see. As a matter of fact, almost anything one does will probably be considered—no matter how
bizarre it may be—as some newfangled practice which is
the norm somewhere or other! Many of the widespread
customs have very dubious historical justification anyway,
and some of them are deplored by purists and scholars of
the history of church ceremonial. My advice to the new-
comer is that if he misses some piece of action in the service
in which the rest of the congregation takes part, he assume
an air of superior knowledge, which will suggest to the
others in the congregation that he is privy to some secret
of ceremonial scholarship of which they in their ignorance
are still not aware! From the days of the first Prayer Book
of Edward VI (1549) there has been a wide toleration of
all kinds of ceremonial practices, a tolerance that finds expression in the quaint language of that Prayer Book: "As
touching kneeling, crossing, holding up of hands, knock-
ing upon the breast, and other gestures: they may be used
or left as every man's devotion serveth without blame."
One may worship in an Episcopal church of the barest
kind of simplicity. The Prayer Book is read without any
embellishments of ceremonial except those which are re-

quired by the rubrics of the service itself. On the other hand, an Episcopal church in the next town, or only a few blocks away, will surround the reading of a service with the most elaborate action and pageantry, complete with incense, bowing, the sign of the cross, holy water, and many other things with which the ordinary Protestant is completely unfamiliar.

This liberty in what every one agrees are non-essentials of Christian worship has, of course, been found in the Church throughout its history. Differences between Eastern and Western Christianity, differences between the usages of the Church at Rome, the Church in Gaul, the Church in Britain, and elsewhere—this variety has always obtained and as long as men differ in taste and outlook it presumably will always continue. If Christians are ever to achieve the reunion of the separated Churches, which we discuss elsewhere in this little book, it can only be by the adoption of some such broad and liberal policy concerning public worship as that which has been a mark of the Anglican tradition. There must be room, for example, for the kind of public worship that celebrates the glory and wonder of God's being and purpose in pageantry and ceremonial which makes use of all His gifts and the uses to which men have put those gifts through their creative artistry.

It has been my privilege in the last few years to live near the great Cathedral of St. John the Divine in New York City. Here the familiar services of the Prayer Book take on new significance, set against the background of a building of breathtaking proportions and boldness of design. The great high points of the Christian Year are celebrated before vast congregations and with dramatic ceremonial which symbolizes the majesty and glory of the God whom we worship. On the other hand, I have had a very different but equally satisfying experience of worship in a simple rural mission in Virginia where without the aid of great vistas of Gothic arches or the thrilling peal of a great organ or the unearthly beauty and purity of a highly trained boys' choir we have simply read the majestic words of the Prayer Book and felt the warmth and intimacy of God's concern with every individual and the sense of His presence wherever two or three are gathered together in His name.

The Episcopal Church's worship as it is now prescribed and carried on is not, of course, a model which the ecumenical church in the future can take over without amendment and enrichment. For example, the Quaker experience of the power and reality of the ministry of silence is not sufficiently provided for in the present formula of Anglican worship. Indeed, there seems to be a kind of conspiracy between the clergy and the organist to fill in even the few moments of necessary silence with some kind of music so that man is never left to confront the reality of his life under God without "something going on." The Anglican tradition does, however, point the way toward the kind of variety which will have to characterize any ecumenical or universal church if it is really to comprehend all the diversified tastes and temperaments that go to make up the human family. By its use of beauty, color, the art and craftsmanship of man, precious metals, movement and pageantry, the Episcopal Church speaks eloquently of a God who sanctifies the best and highest aspirations and achievements of the human spirit, accepting and using all that mankind has to offer Him and blessing and converting mankind thereby. It was this instinct in the Episcopal Church that commended her to me from our first acquaintance and which continues to inspire and delight me as I live and worship in her tradition.

FIVE

"WITH ALL THY MIND"

A S EARLY as my Confirmation class I found the Episcopal Church to be extraordinarily liberal and broad
in its appreciation of the role of man's intellect and reason
in his Christian life. It was the mid-Twenties, and the
Fundamentalist-Modernist controversy was raging everywhere. I was not a very well-informed or passionate rebel—
but I *was* rebellious, with the awe-inspiring conviction of
the young that my own opinions were of inestimable importance. To my great relief the theological requirements
of the Episcopal Church as they were presented to me in
that Confirmation class were minimal and had to do with
basic affirmations of belief. Somehow the recitation of the
Apostles' or the Nicene Creed in public worship with the
rest of the congregation did not disturb me very much—
although I personally would have preferred some editing
of specific phrases. I did not learn until much later of the
form in which the Creeds are repeated among the Eastern

76

Orthodox Christians: *"We* believe. . . ." Even though I was obliged to repeat the Creed in the first person singular, I did so in the company of the whole congregation, and this somehow took much of the burden of personal comprehension and conviction off my own shoulders. The Creeds were like the Pledge of Allegiance to the Flag—a statement of the platform of this society and community. I was willing to accept it as such even though I continued to have some minor difficulties with specific phrases. Of which more later. I still would say to the doubter or the inquirer who finds the Creed a stumbling block, "Do you believe the main thing . . . that God is in Christ offering us His love and His pardon? If so, trust the Church's wisdom for the detailed way that fundamental faith has been expressed. This was *her* faith before it was *yours*. Some day you will see it her way."

I have already described my relief when the rector in a casual remark to the Confirmation class observed that as long as one was able to say "I believe in God the Father, Creator of heaven and earth," he was perfectly free to accept any version of the manner in which the creation was accomplished which science suggested to be true. The sanity and wisdom of this approach to the Bible appealed to me greatly. I did not know then what I know now, namely that behind this casual remark in Confirmation class lay a long history of Anglicanism with its distinctive understanding of the role of Scripture in Christian thought and life. Because this history has had much to do with freeing the Anglican from the bitterness of the controversy over the Bible that has raged in other Christian circles, perhaps it deserves some brief summary here.

The great Anglican theologian, Richard Hooker, writing toward the end of the reign of Queen Elizabeth I, was confronted in the Puritan movement with a totalitarian and authoritarian version of the Scriptures and their place in the Christian Church. Under the leadership of Thomas Cartwright, Lady Margaret Professor of Divinity at Cambridge University, the Puritan movement had taken the position that even in the details of her worship and governmental organization the Church was bound to strict obedience to the laws of God as revealed in the Bible. Hooker's *Laws of Ecclesiastical Polity* attacked this contention by insisting that the Bible was not the only place where God's laws could be discovered. God also makes His laws known to us through our reason, operating on the evidence of our senses and of history. The Bible has as its single task, according to Hooker, the declaration of the saving purpose of God in Christ and the necessity for trusting in Him as the center and ground of Christian discipleship.

To make clear this crucial Christian revelation, the Bible is for Hooker all-important and all-sufficient. A wide range of questions, however, find no conclusive answer in Scripture at all. Some of these questions are practical ones, having to do with the relation of the Church to the State, the internal government of the Church, the ceremonial embellishment of the Church's worship, and many others. Some are of a theological character. For example, the nature of the presence of Christ in the Holy Communion is regarded by Hooker as a matter on which the Bible does not speak definitively, at least not in detail with respect to its mode or manner. A whole range of questions on which the Bible throws no direct light are primarily cultural or intellectual in character. The nature and processes of the physical world, the constitution and functioning of human society, the whole cultural and historical development of mankind—all of these have for Hooker a kind of autonomous importance. As man thinks about these questions, using his faculties of observation and reason, he is in a very real sense, according to Hooker, discovering some of the laws of God.

The result of this repudiation of the exclusive role of the Bible as the only guide for the Christian man meant that Anglicanism was prepared to assign enormous importance to man's cultural and intellectual activities. This reflected itself in the encouragement given to the growth and development of the two great English universities, Cambridge and Oxford. Both of them took seriously the obligations of churchmanship and yet left free the ranging curiosity of the human intellect, believing that no honest and conscientious use of the mind of man will disclose anything but further truth about God. As a result of this tradition, the Anglican vicar has often combined with his spiritual duties some intellectual hobby which may, as a matter of fact, qualify him as something of a world expert in his particular field of interest and study. Whatever disadvantages this breadth of interest has involved—and it must be confessed that it has sometimes meant a kind of ivory tower academic seclusion from the practical concerns of the laity of the Church—it has meant nevertheless that Anglicanism has been one of the most congenial spiritual homes for men and women of broad intellectual interests and sympathies.

In theology, this broad platform of intellectual interest
has meant a wider and keener interest in historical theology
than has been characteristic of most other Christian
churches. The Anglican theologian is not content with
the exposition of some Biblical text. He will insist on
bringing to bear also the wisdom and insights of the
Church Fathers. In the beginning of the Reformation this
wide interest in the Church's great theological tradition
—especially its pre-mediaeval version—was characteristic of
almost all the leading Protestant thinkers. The great Elizabethan divine, John Jewel, corresponded regularly with
his friends in the Swiss churches, and the correspondence
was filled with learned references to Cyprian, Augustine,
Ambrose and the other worthies of the Patristic period.
As Protestantism developed, however, it became the special
hallmark of Anglicanism to be concerned with the long
and rich tradition of Christian thought. At least in part,
this may have resulted in a lack of careful attention to
the analysis of Biblical themes and texts. The Scotch Presbyterian or the continental Protestant was often more illuminating in his treatment of the Bible than was his
Anglican brother. On the other hand, his Anglican coun-
terpart was often broader and more inclusive in his concerns with human life and human history.

At least one notable advantage of the Anglican approach and treatment of theology appeared in the crisis
over higher criticism of the Bible which broke over the
Christian church in the 19th and early 20th centuries.
Like any other group of people, Anglicanism in general
and the Episcopal Church in America in particular, had
its full quota of conservatives—perhaps a little more than

its full quota—and there was a widespread sense of shock
and dismay at the implications of the new discoveries
about the ways in which the Bible had been written and
given its present form. It is notable, however, that at least
in America the so-called Fundamentalist Movement had
less success and importance in the Episcopal Church than
in any other major Protestant body. Since the Anglican
ethos had always emphasized the authority of the Church
and of its age-long tradition as the interpreter of Scripture, the discovery that wholly new modes of interpretation of Scripture were required by the discoveries of the
higher critics dismayed Anglicans less than most other
Protestants. Familiarity with the Church Fathers, for example, had already taught Anglicans that there was more
than one way to read the Bible and more than one sense
in which any given passage might be taken. The wide use
of allegory, for example, suggested that Christians in different periods of the Church's history might use Scripture
in quite different ways. What was more obvious than that
in our time Scripture would have to be employed with
new methods of interpretation?

The use of the Apostles' and Nicene Creeds as the statements of faith in the Episcopal Book of Common Prayer
had always served to give perspective to the Bible and to
hold up for special attention the great central story of
God's dealings with man which the Bible represents. Without this guidance it would have been much easier for
Anglicanism to fall into a kind of textual Bibliolatry. To
question the accuracy, for example, of the opening chapters of the Book of Genesis as an historical description of
the ways in which the creation of the world came about

would, of course, be initially a shock to a traditionally
minded Episcopalian as much as to a member of any other
of the main Christian traditions. But after the initial shock
had passed, the Episcopalian might recall that the historic
creeds had never said more than that God was ultimately
responsible for bringing into being "all things visible and
invisible." If this is the *main* thing which we learn from
the Book of Genesis, then perhaps it is not so crucial to
believe that the process of creation took place in just
exactly the manner in which it is there recounted. Growing up as I did in an age of widespread skepticism about
the Bible, it was important beyond estimation to find that
the Episcopal Church had long since laid hold of a few
basic Biblical themes as being central and important and
that one could concentrate his spiritual and intellectual
energies in the consideration of these great matters rather
than undertaking the impossible task of defending every
word of the Bible as infallibly and literally true.

The use of the historic creeds has, of course, posed some
problems of conscience and scruple for modern men and
women. The creeds admittedly employ what it is now
fashionable to call "mythological" language. A cosmology
in which God "comes down" from heaven, and "ascends"
up into it again, and a conception of one of the Persons
of the Triune God sitting "on the right hand" of the
other, has troubled many modern people. Of course, this
is a problem for any Christian Church that regards the
Bible as having any authority whatever in the establishment of doctrine. The important role given in Anglicanism
to the use of reason leads, however, to a recognition of the
essentially poetic and mythological character of such lan-

guage. Somewhat more difficult, however—at least for me —has been the inclusion of the reference to the Virgin Birth of our Lord in the creed. I am convinced that the true genius of Anglicanism requires us to treat this question as one of historical evidence and therefore to leave the way open for the individual Episcopalian to doubt it or to affirm it, depending upon the way in which the evidence strikes him. Scholars agree that the Church put the phrase "born of the Virgin Mary" into the creed not in order to insist upon the virginal conception of our Lord but rather to insist upon the fact that He had a human mother and was therefore fully a human being and also that His birth came about by God's initiating activity. I would agree with one of our leading contemporary Anglican theologians, Professor J. V. Langmead Casserley, that "it is undeniably true that the historical evidence of the Virgin Birth, although it certainly exists and is not without its weight, is inconclusive." * I cannot follow Professor Casserley, however, in his conviction that "the Virgin Birth presents an issue too deeply embedded in the Christian tradition and too relevant to matters basically affecting the Christian decision of faith for the whole question to be left in indefinite abeyance." If evidence is inconclusive, there is no alternative for a man who is concerned for the integrity of his reason but to leave the question "in indefinite abeyance."

This exhibition of differences within the Anglican Community will, perhaps, teach the outsider something of the nature of our unity. Obviously no one can be an Episcopalian who does not accept the doctrine of the Trinity

* *The Living Church.* Vol. 134, No. 1, January 6, 1957, page 6.

and the Incarnation. What cannot, however, be required
is any decision on what is essentially a matter of historical
evidence, namely, the way in which the Incarnation took
place in terms of specific historical events. That in Jesus
Christ we see God come in the flesh is of the essence of
the creeds and indeed of the New Testament itself. To
dogmatize, however, on a matter where evidence must be
determinative seems to me a very un-Anglican thing to do.
To assure the reader that I speak here for a substantial
number of Anglicans, I would refer him to a book issued
some time ago in the Church of England which reports the
following situation with respect to the attitude toward this
question in that Mother Church of Anglicanism: "Many
of us hold . . . that belief in the Word made flesh is in-
tegrally bound up with belief in the Virgin Birth . . . there
are, however, some among us who hold that a full belief
in the historical Incarnation is more consistent with the
supposition that our Lord's birth took place under the
normal conditions of human generation . . . We . . . recog-
nize that both the views outlined . . . are held by members
of the Church . . . who fully accept the reality of our Lord's
Incarnation, which is the central truth of the Christian
faith." * The fact is that at the present time the theological situation in the Episcopal Church is marked both by
an increasing agreement on the central issues of the Christian faith and by a continuing difference of opinion about
just which affirmations are to be considered as central!
Anglicanism is hesitant about premature dogmatism and

* *Doctrine in the Church of England.* Macmillan, New York, 1938.
Page 82-83.

prefers to leave questions such as these to be resolved by further study and prayer.

I was also attracted by the modesty of the claims of Anglican theology. It was obvious that here was no rigid theological blueprint, no attempt to "unscrew the inscrutable." The mystery and incomprehensibility of God was reflected in the Church's lack of precision and definition at many points. I was impressed with the amount of reverent agnosticism that was permitted in this version of Christianity. Wide differences of points of view were obviously allowed on matters which had rent asunder other communions and church traditions. No single Christian thinker dominated the Anglican theological scene. We were not called to believe in Hookerism or Cranmerism. Indeed it has always seemed to me that Anglicanism lacks any official theology. The Bible alone, illuminated by two thousand years of Christian thought, is the only theological platform to which the Episcopal Church is fully committed. It is true that the 39 Articles of Religion have had an authoritative position in Anglicanism since their formulation in the 16th Century. However, an examination of the 39 Articles reveals that they are content simply to reiterate Biblical themes and ideas, and indeed make the flat assertion that "Holy Scripture containeth all things necessary to salvation." The historic creeds themselves are justified in the 39 Articles only on the ground that "they may be proved by most certain warrants of Holy Scripture" (Article 8, *Of the Creeds*). The Church's authority in interpreting Scripture is affirmed (Article 20, *Of the Authority of the Church:* "The Church hath . . . authority in Controversies of Faith"). On the other hand this authority is plainly

limited ("it is not lawful for the Church to ordain anything that is contrary to God's Word written, neither may
it so expound one place of Scripture, that it be repugnant
to another").

What is perhaps most striking about the 39 Articles is
that in some of the deep matters of the Christian faith
there is a parsimony of words and a modesty of theological
ambition. The great Biblical idea of election and predestination, for example, is treated in Article 17, but how
different this Article is from the decisions of the famous
Synod of Dort, the latter reflecting an attempt to press
the definition of God's sovereignty to the point of eliminat-
ing man's freedom and responsibility. The Article on
Predestination and Election follows closely the Christian
experience of St. Paul as that is recorded in the Epistle to
the Romans. All Christians know that they have been
"called" into whatever Christian understanding or virtue
they possess.

Anyone who reflects at all about the course of his life
knows how much of what has been precious and valuable
has simply been given to him. The introductory chapter of
this little book bears witness to a widespread human experience, namely, that some of the most important relationships of my life come about not through my choice but
through the intervention and gift of others. The Christian
interprets these experiences as the guiding and leading of
the providence of God. Why am I a Christian while my
friend who is obviously intellectually and spiritually my
superior is not? This was the real problem which confronted St. Paul, for example, and led him to his discussion
of the doctrine of election and predestination. The only

answer can be, I believe, that God in His infinite wisdom and knowledge about the workings of the human will and mind has made known to me what he has not yet for some strange reason made known to my friend, namely, the unsearchable riches of Christ.

Article 17 says something very much like this and finds that "the godly consideration" of this fact of God's gift of insight and power is the heart and motivation of all Christian life. This is not a doctrine, however, to be thundered abroad to the unbeliever—or, as the Article puts it, to "curious and carnal persons, lacking the spirit of Christ." In other words, to press the doctrine of election and predestination in such a way as to deny man's responsibility and freedom goes far beyond the meaning that the doctrine holds in the Bible itself. Likewise any interpretation of predestination which denies God's universal love for mankind—or as the Article puts it, "God's promises . . . as they be *generally* (italics mine) set forth in Holy Scripture"—is carefully guarded against. Such is the modesty of the Anglican treatment of one of the theological doctrines that has caused schisms and heartaches throughout wide areas of Christendom.

The result of this refusal to develop an official theology has been that Anglicanism has never suffered any major doctrinal schisms. The defection from the American Episcopal Church of a small group of clergy and laity in the mid-nineteenth century over the issue of baptismal regeneration proved to be numerically insignificant, and the resulting Reformed Episcopal Church has never spread far beyond a few of the larger cities of the eastern seaboard. Outsiders find this breadth and tolerance difficult to believe, and one is often asked questions like: "Are you a High Church Episcopalian or a Low Church Episcopalian?" Such a questioner often assumes that these differences are hard and fast ones, representing almost distinct branches within the Episcopal Church as a whole. Nothing, of course, could be farther from the truth. Very few dioceses and very few parishes are of a "monochrome" type, representing, that is, only one kind of theological slant. As a matter of fact, the very terms "Low Church" and "High Church" have had such a complicated development in meaning that their usefulness in describing even present tendencies within the thought and life of the Episcopal Church is highly questionable. The "High Churchman" of 1688, for example, is certainly not identical either in theology or in ceremonial with the Anglo-Catholic of the modern day. All that one can say is that there have been in the history of Anglicanism a variety of theologies and that today at least three such tendencies can be observed.

There is, in the first place, the Anglo-Catholic Movement. Its main interest is to stress both in its theology and ceremonial the continuity of the present-day Church with the Holy Catholic Church in all the ages since our Lord's Resurrection and Ascension. In this stress and emphasis it has been conservative and historical, especially—by contrast with other tendencies in the Episcopal Church—with respect to the life and customs both of Eastern Orthodoxy and of the mediaeval Western Church. At the hands of a very small minority of its leaders it has sometimes seemed to take on an authoritarian rigidity which is, ironically enough, reminiscent most of all of the attitude of the Puritan party in the Elizabethan Church. Like the Puritans of old, some few modern Anglo-Catholics assume that they and they alone represent the true genius of Anglicanism, and they are willing to tolerate other points of view only in the hope of their eventual conversion. The greater majority of Anglo-Catholics, however, would rejoice in the diversity of the Anglican Communion, provided that such diversity did not tolerate departure from basic Catholic doctrine. In many ways the Anglo-Catholic Movement within the Episcopal Church fulfills the function of a Conservative Party in a political spectrum. It is unwilling to see that which has behind it the weight of hundreds of years of tradition lightly cast aside. It reminds the religious worshipper that he is never "on his own" and that it is never quite true, as many like to claim, that anyone "has his own religion." Christianity is embedded in history, and the Anglo-Catholic Movement reminds us that, far from having "my own religion," we have a religion which has met and responded to all manner of situations and circumstances, has witnessed the rise and fall of empires, has ministered to men in their adversity as well as in their prosperity, has tamed and subdued civilizations and peoples and has stood steadfast and unbending under the bludgeoning of persecution. All Episcopalians, whether they call themselves Anglo-Catholics or not, show something of the marks of this great movement and tendency of thought in their religious attitude and outlook.

There is, in the second place, the Evangelical Movement. Its main concern has been to emphasize the original Christian experience as it is recorded in the New Testament, recovered in the Protestant Reformation, proclaimed powerfully and eloquently in the Wesleyan Revival in England in the 18th and early 19th centuries, and vividly relevant today when men are once again asking deep questions of the meaning of their personal existence in a strangely hostile and threatening world. For the Evangelical, Christianity is primarily the personal acceptance of God's love in Christ as the ground and assurance of His forgiveness, acceptance and status as a son of God. The favorite themes of Evangelical preaching are the devastating and ruinous effects of sin in the life of man and the unbounded and overflowing love of God as evidenced in the life and death and resurrection of His Son. The great Christian succession, according to the Evangelical, runs from St. Paul through St. Augustine to Luther and Calvin to John Wesley and Charles Simeon and presently to such modern Evangelicals as Bryan Green. The Evangelical would remind his Anglo-Catholic brother that God is "able of these stones to raise up children unto Abraham" and that no trust can be put in anything less than God's forgiving and enabling love. The Church is important but chiefly as the appointed means by which individual men and women are brought to accept their status as forgiven sinners, wholly dependent upon the mercy and grace of God. The presence of the Evangelical Movement in the Church of England is a sure witness to the fact that Anglicanism shares fully in the tradition of the Protestant Reformation. The Anglo-Catholic Movement would stress the continuity of the Church of England with the Catholic Church in all ages; the Evangelical Movement would insist on the perennial necessity for judging the Church's life by the supreme test of whether or not it is bearing witness to the unconditional love of God for penitent sinners.

Until a decade or two ago, many observers would have said that the Evangelical Movement was the weakest of the three schools of thought within Anglicanism, that it had conspicuously failed to win the allegiance and excite the interest of the younger clergy and that its power lay chiefly in some vested interests by which it continued to exert a disproportionate influence in the Church. That has all changed, I believe, with the rapid resurgence in English-speaking Christianity of what is called loosely "neo-orthodoxy." I myself found the position of this group of thinkers mightily persuasive in my seminary days, and I have found them so ever since. Paul Tillich, Reinhold Niebuhr, Karl Barth, Emil Brunner and, a hundred years ahead of them all, Soren Kierkegaard—a strange company of theological bedfellows to anyone who knows the details of their many sharp differences and even contradictions—have all, however, made at least this single impact upon modern Christianity: they force us to take seriously the full dimensions of the human problem of alienation, of lostness, of anxiety, of broken-ness, of inner contradiction . . . or to use an often misunderstood Christian word, "sin." None of the leaders is an Anglican, but then none of the chief Protestant Reformers was an Anglican either. True —there had to arise finally a Richard Hooker who could delineate a distinctively Anglican understanding of the Reformation theology. In our day, no such theological giant has made his appearance among us, and we are like the Church of England in the early years of the reign of Elizabeth I—dependent for our greatest theological stimulation on thinkers from outside our own fellowship. This very open-ness, this very humility, this very willingness to be taught by other communions and other traditions is an authentic part of the Anglican genius. We like to claim the adjective "moderate" and to speak of a "via media"— a middle way between two extremes. But in some periods of Anglicanism the initial impulse of thought that was "moderated" came from outside and had first to be fully felt and its validity largely accepted, and the "middle way" was between positions that were strongly represented by opposing schools of thought. There is no single Anglican theological position; there is only a distinctively Anglican theological method. I am glad to be a member of such a supple theological tradition, which can now in our own time make large room for what contemporary Protestant theology has to teach and tell us, even as it has room also for the best in Thomas Aquinas or Duns Scotus or behind them, Augustine. The Evangelical school of thought in Anglicanism is having a genuine revival in our own generation.

More difficult to describe and to differentiate from the other two movements that have been mentioned above is the Broad Church or Liberal Movement in Anglicanism. Here the emphasis is on the continuity between man's religious life and interests and the rest of his existence. Drawing upon the insights of Hooker and, behind him, of the Renaissance tradition exemplified in Erasmus and John Colet, the emphasis of this school of thought has been upon the importance of man's reason and of its use in all manner of intellectual and cultural activities as a genuine part of his offering of himself to God. Broad Churchmen have been sympathetic to the social and intellectual developments of their time, seeking to identify the

Christian Church with all that is best in the contemporary society. The responsibilities implied in the title "The Church of England" have been interpreted by the Broad Churchmen to mean a concern that the Church play a creative and formative role in the nation's total life. Not the Church's continuity with its own past (the Anglo-Catholic concern) nor the Church's foundation in a personal religious experience of forgiveness and new power for life (the Evangelical emphasis) but the role of the Christian Church as expressing and consecrating all that is noblest and finest and most enlightened in man's thinking and aspirations—this is the main stress of a Broad Churchman.

Obviously taken by itself each of these movements betrays some weaknesses. The Anglo-Catholic may become a rigid authoritarian; the Evangelical may become a sentimental individualist; the Broad Churchman may become an amiable reflection of the presuppositions of his immediate environment. Taken together, however, in a continuing encounter with each other, these three movements help to keep Anglicanism alive to the present, loyal to the past, and sensitive to man's utter dependence upon God's love and mercy. The late Archbishop of York, Dr. Cyril F. Garbett, in an address at the General Convention of the Episcopal Church in 1949, put it this way: "Anglicanism stands not for tolerance for the sake of compromise but for comprehension for the sake of truth." In a time when men are tempted to grasp for any easy religious reassurance, even one which involves the abdication of intellectual responsibility, and which turns away from the consideration of present-day human problems in an escape to some ivory-

tower shrine of personal religious security, I am gladder
than ever that I am an Episcopalian. I am glad that I
belong to a tradition which is modest and reasonable in its
approach to religious truth, that is many-sided and rich
in its appreciation of the religious character of every aspect
of man's existence, that is emphatic in its focus upon man's
sin and God's love as the center of the Christian religion.

SIX

THE LAW OF LIBERTY

EVERY Episcopalian in his Confirmation is made aware by the presence and central responsibility of the Bishop in the Confirmation Service of the continuity of his own Christian life and that of the particular congregation to which he seeks to belong with an authoritative tradition, reaching back to the days of the Apostles themselves. On the other hand, he soon discovers that he has been taken up into an extraordinarily democratic church organization where each man's voice can be heard and where the free processes of discussion, deliberation and decision formulate major policy.

In some respects the polity of the Episcopal Church corresponds to the political situation in England. We find there, on the one hand, the greatest imaginable respect for democratic processes and for the freedom of the individual to speak his mind and to express his convictions. On the other hand, however, there is a deeply rooted respect for the Crown—albeit vaguely defined—which gives continuity and stability to the national society. It would be misleading, of course, to suggest that the Bishop is no more than a constitutional monarch, but the analogy is suggestive and illuminating. This unique combination of freedom and authority, representing a creative merging of ancient ecclesiastical tradition with modern political insight, is one of the important reasons why many people are drawn to the Episcopal Church and find it a most congenial spiritual home.

This combination of freedom and authority, of course, has its roots in the Bible itself. It is abundantly clear in the New Testament, for example, that freedom and liberty are essential and distinguishing marks of the Christian life. In the writings of St. Paul especially, one of the chief contrasts is between the new Israel, which is the Christian Church, and the old Israel on this very matter of freedom and liberty. St. Paul frequently distinguishes the freedom and responsibility which the individual Christian enjoys in his relationship to God from the inhibited and enslaved kind of relationship which, he believed, was characteristic of Judaism. "For freedom Christ has set us free," he writes to the Galatians, "stand fast, therefore, and do not submit again to the yoke of slavery" (Galatians 5:1). The use of the phrase "sons of God" establishes as the ideal of the Christian life a mature and responsible liberty. No Christianity which is consistent with the New Testament can set up as its ideal any kind of blind subservience or unquestioning obedience.

Although this point is made most clearly in the Pauline epistles, it must be noted that the whole manner and

method of our Lord's ministry point in the same direction.
It is a ministry of powerful effectiveness but marked by
surprising reticence. No boastful claims are made about
His special messianic character. Indeed, in St. Mark's
Gospel, it is notable that He forbids any widespread publication of the success of His healing ministry, presumably
on the grounds that He would not by such means coerce
or beguile an awestruck and overwhelmed following. It has
been pointed out also that the parables make great demands on the perception and insight of the individual.
They may be taken simply as attractive and charming
stories, and any man is free to hear them on that level
alone. On the other hand, "he that hath ears to hear, let
him hear." The man who would probe more deeply, seeking in these deceptively simple stories a clue to the meaning
of life and the nature of God, will have his reward. Discipleship for Jesus was always a highly personal decision,
involving oftentimes radical separation from one's tradition and background (hence the repetition of the injunction to leave father and mother, if necessary). Perhaps no
other great religion of mankind makes as great a demand
and sets as high a value on the individual believer as does
Christianity.

On the other hand, the New Testament is full of discussions of the concept of authority. It was one of the predominant notes of the ministry of Christ, and we read that
"with authority commandeth He even the unclean spirits
and they do obey Him." (Luke 4:36) What is more, this
same authority is bestowed upon His followers. "Then He
called His twelve disciples together and gave them power
and authority over all devils and to cure diseases. And He

sent them to preach the Kingdom of God and to heal the
sick." (Luke 9:1 and 2) It has been pointed out that the
same Greek word—*exousia*—can be translated both "authority" and also "power." That is to say, the New Testament recognizes that authority is always linked with
effective power. We make the same connection in English
when we speak, for example, of someone who plays the
piano "with authority." This means that the pianist in
question has a command of the techniques and possibilities
of the instrument by reason of capacities and abilities. So
authority in the New Testament is not so much legalis-
tically asserted as it is effectively demonstrated. The authority which was given to the disciples, for example, was
manifested in the power of their message and ministry to
release man from the bondage of sin and to give him the
power to lead the Christian life in trust and in love. This
power, of course, is ultimately ascribed to God alone.
Again and again in the Book of the Acts of the Apostles
it is insisted that because the Holy Spirit was at work
through the life and fellowship and mission of the Apostolic Church it had, therefore, an authority and power to
accomplish God's work and purpose among men. The
Apostolic Church had authority, "being full of the Holy
Ghost."

The concern of the early Church in developing authoritative forms and orders within its life was precisely that
the liberating message of the Gospel and all its power and
effectiveness might everywhere be heard and believed and
practiced. The development of the monarchical episcopacy
(that is, the authoritative rule of one bishop in each large
community), of the canon of Scripture, of the creeds and

other formulations of the ecumenical councils—all these were designed to safeguard the original integrity and power of the Christian message rather than to establish some legalistic and authoritarian structure to which individual Christians were to be blindly and unquestioningly subservient. The more one reads the history of the first four centuries of the Church the more one is impressed with the caution and reserve with which authoritarian structures were developed. The great decisions of the ecumenical councils, for example, did, of course, rule out certain misunderstandings of the Christian message, but equally impressive is the fact that they are allowed large room for varieties of understanding and interpretation. The descriptions that we have of church life of the time suggest no oppressive and tyrannous despotism on the part of the bishops but, for the most part, (though one must confess that there are distressing exceptions) a willingness to leave much freedom and much independence to individual clergy and congregations and even to individual believers.

It is not possible here to discuss the ways in which this original Christian conception of authority became in other periods and circumstances corrupted by serious abuse. It is sufficient to say that the Anglican Reformation sought to recover this ancient conception of authority as designed primarily to secure the achievement of freedom and liberty for the Christian man. It is perhaps difficult to commend this Anglican settlement to American readers who are familiar with the principle of separation of Church and State. It must be granted that the Elizabethan religious settlement knew no such principle and that it employed the power of the State to secure religious conformity. We should not let our disappointment with this failure of the fathers of the English Reformation to appreciate fully the principle of religious toleration lead us to overlook the significance of the forward step in the achievement of a balance between authority and liberty which the English Reformation does demonstrate. The participation of the Crown and of Parliament in the religious decisions of the English nations is of the greatest significance. Not only the bishops and higher clergy were asked to determine questions of the form of the Prayer Book, the number of dioceses, and other important ecclesiastical questions, but these were matters for prolonged parliamentary debate and for consideration by the Crown and its counsellors.

At the same time, it was recognized that the great central matters of the Christian faith were not, of course, subject to revision or amendment. Anglican respect for tradition precluded any radical innovations in matters which Christians had always regarded as crucial, necessary and central. The role of the bishops and other clergy in preaching and administering the Sacraments was generally recognized and safeguarded. It is true that hot-headed Tudor and Stuart monarchs and equally hot-headed Parliaments sometimes overstepped the boundaries in such matters which the general consensus of the English Church had established. Archbishop Laud refers in some of his writings to the unfortunate example of the Emperor Constantius who, as he says, "meddled in determining, and that beforehand, what the prelates should do . . . but then we must know withal, that Athanasius reckoned him for this, as that antichrist which Daniel prophesied of!" The

teaching function of the clergy and more especially of the
episcopate held its ground even against the proud bluster-
ings of Parliament or the monarchy. There are limits to
democracy in any Church which can claim the name of
Christian. The authentic Christian Gospel is not established by a majority vote; it comes down from two thousand years of Christian experience and testimony which
has overwhelming weight and authority. What is significant, however, is that this weight and authority are freely
acknowledged and accepted by representative assemblies
drawn from both the clerical and lay orders of the Church.
This important idea was insisted upon in the Anglican
Reformation and formed a basis for the even more thoroughgoing democratization of the Church which took
place in America.

It has often been observed that the fathers of the American Constitution were also the fathers of the Constitution
and Canons of the Episcopal Church in America. Their
wisdom is equally evident in both documents. On the one
hand, laymen are invited to share in all the deliberative,
judicial and administrative functions of the Church. When
first introduced, these proposals brought forth a storm of
disapproval. Most offensive to the traditionalist was the
suggestion that laymen could sit on trial courts for the discipline and possible deposition of presbyters and bishops.
One shocked comment of the period, reflecting social snob-
bery perhaps as much as ecclesiastical conservatism, specu-
lated that the bishop's barber might shave him in the
morning "and in the afternoon vote him out of his office."
Despite such opposition, however, the right of the layman
to participate at all levels of the Church's legislative, ex-

ecutive and judicial life was strongly affirmed. Great authority and responsibility were vested in the parish congregation, which in turn elected a vestry and delegates to a diocesan convention. So strong was the democratic tide in the early days of America that in many Atlantic seaboard dioceses the bishop was not even allowed to enter a church to perform ecclesiastical or sacramental acts without the invitation and consent of the vestry or the rector! The laity of the Church may exercise a decisive veto both in the diocesan and general conventions of the Church. A "vote by orders" means that both the clergy and the laity, voting separately, must give a concurrent majority if a measure is to pass.

The principle of "checks and balances" also operates in the functioning of the episcopacy. A careful reading of the Constitution and Canons of the Episcopal Church and of most of its constituent dioceses will reveal that the bishop, for example, is able to do very few things on his own sole authority. Again and again he is obliged to secure the consent of this or that committee or group of advisers before his action can be taken as authoritative. No man can be ordained, for example, without a long series of approvals and recommendations in which the laity of the Church by their designated representatives must participate. Although the bishop is given the authority of extending the work of the Church within the boundaries of his own diocese, the clergy and laity control the budgetary and financial support of such work, and therefore participate in the development of policy and program. The laity of the Episcopal Church may exercise the power of veto in all changes in the liturgy, in the election of bishops and on

many other centrally important matters in church life.
Obviously the Episcopal Church, reflecting the spirit and
ideals of the American Constitution, is thoroughly democratic and representative in its life and government.

This important role of the laity in the life and government of the Church involves, of course, important responsibilities for each layman. He is always, except in the most
unusual circumstances, a member of some particular congregation. When he is confirmed he is enrolled in the list
of his congregation and as soon as he is an adult has the
right and responsibility of taking part in the major decisions which the congregation makes, especially through the
election of members of the vestry. The parish is incorpo-
rated under the laws of the state in which it exists, and to
the whole assembly of members of the parish is given the
ultimate responsibility of determining the constitution and
by-laws of the parish corporation under which the vestry
functions. To the vestry is given, in most dioceses of the
country, almost complete authority in the calling of a
rector. In some dioceses the bishop participates in the selection, and in all dioceses he must give his consent before any
final choice is made.

The vestry or parish meeting also elects delegates to a
diocesan convention, which, as we have said, is the supreme
legislative authority in a diocese. There are 75 dioceses in
the Protestant Episcopal Church and 27 missionary districts, the latter being states or parts of states or over-seas
territories where the Church is not yet sufficiently strong
to be self-supporting. In the case of self-supporting dioceses,
the diocesan convention has the sole authority and responsibility for electing its bishop. In a large diocese assistant

bishops are sometimes needed, and again to the diocesan convention is left the responsibility of providing such assistance if the bishop of the diocese requests it and the convention believes his request is justified. Again, however, the principle of "checks and balances" operates, and no diocese is allowed either to elect any particular man as its bishop or to determine that it needs assistant bishops without the approval of other bishops and other dioceses. This insures that only broadly representative men who command the respect of the whole Church can be elevated to these important positions of leadership.

Each diocese and missionary district elects delegates to the supreme legislative authority of the Protestant Episcopal Church, namely, the General Convention. Here, following the manner of the United States Constitution, two legislative houses are provided for and must concur in any legislation. As has also been pointed out already, the laity and the clergy who make up the House of Deputies may with proper parliamentary procedure require separate voting so that both laity and clergy must concur. In the General Convention is vested the ultimate responsibility for the development of the Constitution and Canon Law of the Church and the promotion and development of its overall missionary program. The House of Bishops, although it can pass no legislation without the concurrence of the House of Deputies, has for many years made it a practice from time to time to issue pastoral letters, dealing with important aspects of Church life or with moral or ethical issues in the life of the Church, the nation, and the world. Such pastoral letters must be read in every congregation of the Church.

The supreme executive official of the Episcopal Church is the Presiding Bishop, chosen by a majority vote of the House of Bishops and confirmed by the majority vote of the House of Deputies. Upon election to this office, he resigns from whatever diocesan position he has held and remains as Presiding Bishop until he reaches the age of 72. His main responsibilities are the direction of the missionary, educational, promotional and social relations aspects of the Church's program, and the presidency of the House of Bishops, in which function he also supervises the arrangements for the certification of election and the consecration of new bishops. Like the Presidency of the United States, the office of Presiding Bishop depends for its power and effectiveness to a very great extent upon the character and leadership of the incumbent in the office. However, in recent years canonical legislation has tended to increase the responsibilities and authority of the Presiding Bishop, so that he is now a much more important person in the eyes of the Church than he was a century ago.

In this thoroughly democratic organization, however, the traditional spiritual prerogatives of the bishops and of the clergy are carefully maintained. Although a clergyman cannot be forced upon a congregation against its will, neither can the congregation dissolve the pastoral relationship between itself and its rector without the bishop's consent and concurrence. As a result, there is a very real respect for the independence and integrity of the clergyman in the exercise of his spiritual duties. I know of no other democratically organized Church in which the freedom of the minister in the pulpit is more carefully safeguarded than in the Episcopal Church. This is not to say

that he does not have difficulties when he espouses un-
popular causes, but he has behind him a certain weight of
tradition as well as the provisions of canon law which
defend and sustain his rights.

This is not only true with respect to his preaching, but
in the very important question of the admission and excommunication of members. It is his responsibility to see
to it that candidates for Baptism and Confirmation are
properly instructed in the elements of the Christian faith
and in their responsibilities as Christians and churchmen.
No Episcopal rector would have the problem which arose
for a friend of mine, a minister of a highly democratically
organized congregation of another Protestant communion,
whose efforts to integrate Negro church members into his
congregation were vetoed by an adverse vote of the congregation. In that very same community, I was able to present
Negro candidates for Baptism and Confirmation, to welcome them at the Communion rail and to integrate them
into the spiritual life of the parish without any questions
being raised about my right to do so. This was done in
spite of the fact that I knew that at least a small number
of the members of my congregation disapproved of this
kind of development of a racially integrated parish. Episcopal clergymen, of course, will in the exercise of these responsibilities want to be "as wise as serpents and harmless
as doves" and will usually try not to get too far ahead of
their congregations in the exercise of their spiritual privileges. This is a part of any clergyman's pastoral responsibility. This freedom, however, does enable him to embody
the prophetic tradition of the Christian ministry even
against rather overwhelming opposition in his congrega-

tion in a way that is scarcely possible when the ministerial
tenure may be revoked by a simple majority of a congregational meeting.

Likewise to the minister, acting under the supervision
of the bishop, is given the awesome responsibility of excommunication. By the rubrics of the Prayer Book two
grounds are established as the basis for any minister re-
pelling from the Holy Communion a confirmed member
of the Church. It is interesting that in both cases the real
ground for excommunication is the possibility of offense
and scandal to the main body of the congregation. This is
specifically stated in the first instance where the ground
for excommunication is that the person is "a notorious and
open evil liver." Why is the emphasis placed on "notorious
and open"? Is discreet secret vice to be condoned? Of course,
the answer is that a flaunting of the Christian ethic and its
standards in a public and open way calls into question the
whole character and ideal of Christian discipleship. Because it threatens to scandalize and disrupt the congregation and to destroy its witness in the world, "notorious
and open" evil living may be a cause for the extreme discipline of excommunication. The other offense is equally
an offense against the nature and character of Christian
discipleship. The minister may repel from the Communion "those, betwixt whom he perceiveth malice and hatred
to reign." Here again the very character and quality of
Christian life is at stake, and the minister may take steps
to safeguard it. In both cases the minister must give notice
to the bishop of any such acts of excommunication, with
the implied suggestion that the bishop will consult and
advise with him about his decisions. Here again it would

seem to be a wise provision which vests responsibilty for
the most serious acts of ecclesiastical discipline, namely, excommunication, in the hands of one who by reason of his
pastoral responsibilities and wisdom will have better
knowledge of background and motives than will the members of a congregation.

In a very similar manner, despite all the checks and
balances the operation of which has been described here as
limiting and defining the role of the bishop in the Church,
there is a genuine and deeply felt respect for the spiritual
responsibilities which the office has traditionally embodied
in the Christian Church. He may have very little legal or
constitutional power; his prestige and moral authority
are, however, incalculable and widely felt. The prophetic
role of some of the bishops of the American Church testi-
fies to the possibilities of the episcopal office, fulfilling in
modern times some of the best elements in the tradition
which stretches from Ambrose to Thomas à Becket to
William Temple.

This respect for the episcopal office does not depend
upon any particular theory about the origin of the episcopal office in the Church. Not all Episcopalians agree in
their theories about how the office of a bishop came to hold
the place it has held in most branches of the Christian
Church since the middle of the second century. All Episcopalians would agree, probably, in affirming the idea of
Apostolic Succession in the sense that the bishop exercises
in the contemporary Church the same role which the
Apostles exercised in the Church of the years immediately
following the Resurrection. Episcopalians differ, however,
as to whether this continuation of influence and responsi-

bility was the result of a direct command of our Lord or whether it developed in the life of the early Church under the guidance of the Holy Spirit. The resolution of this question has seemed to many Episcopalians—of which I would count myself one—to be in large part a question of historical evidence. Since the historical evidence in question is in some ways inconclusive, it has never seemed to me to be possible to make a necessary dogma out of what can only be a tentative historical hypothesis. It is interesting to notice that in the early debates of Elizabethan Anglicans with Puritan opponents over the question of the place of the bishop in the Church, it was the Puritans and not the Anglicans who sought to fix the answer to the question by means of resort to Biblical texts. Many Anglican apologists were willing to say that the role of the bishop in the Church was developed not as a result of our Lord's command but as a convenient and reasonable arrangement of church life which could be justified by its ability to secure the unity and continuity of the Church.

To an Anglican, nearly two centuries of tradition carries its own persuasiveness. The values and importance of the Episcopal office can, however, be demonstrated in terms of present-day effectiveness. There are, for example, obvious advantages to investing authority and symbolizing continuity in a single person. The success of the Episcopal Church in America, for example, in avoiding endless divisions and schisms over relatively obscure points of theology or because of geographical and cultural differences is impressive especially by contrast with the proliferation of groups holding to a congregational or presbyterian type of polity. One of the most notable instances of this success was the reunion of the Northern and Southern Episcopal dioceses immediately after the close of the Civil War. Although, of course, the Southern states organized an Episcopal Church in the Confederacy, it completely disappeared and Southern Churchmen found their way back into union with their Northern brethren within a few years of Appomattox. Only one sizable group of Episcopalians, the so-called Reformed Episcopal Church, has ever separated itself from the main body of the Episcopal Church in the history of America, and that separated body has had such a limited growth that most Episcopalians are not even aware that it exists. Part of the reason for this remarkable maintenance of unity and solidarity in a vast and sprawling nation with strong inclinations toward independence of action and thinking is due almost entirely to the importance that is ascribed to the office of the bishop. The ancient injunction of St. Ignatius, "do nothing without the bishop," has maintained the unified and Catholic conception of the Church in the midst of many tensions and differences both theological and cultural.

Surely one of the most important reasons why I am an Episcopalian is that I have found here a Church which seems to me to make great room for the truths of democracy and of congregational initiative and responsibility and has at the same time defended the spiritual integrity of the ministry and maintained the spiritual unity of the Church through the retention of the age-old conceptions of ministerial and more especially episcopal authority.

SEVEN

"THY NEIGHBOR AS THYSELF"

IN THE MIDST of the turbulent social crises which
shook and challenged the United States during my college years, it was inevitable that my relationship to the
Episcopal Church should be judged in part upon the
quality of social thinking and social action which that
Church seemed to me to demonstrate. To the outsider the
Episcopal Church has often been represented as being
composed almost exclusively of the very wealthy, aristo-
cratic and, as a result, highly conservative members of
society. It may be true that in some places it does bear that
aspect, although my own experience has been that this
characterization of the Episcopal Church is almost everywhere a caricature of the facts. I admit that I was somewhat shaken during the 30's to read indictments of the
Episcopal Church by men like Upton Sinclair, and I
remember sharing his sense of shock at the fact that the
wife of one of the prominent bishops of the Church in the

111

early 1900's had reported to the police a loss of more than $25,000. in jewelry! Mr. Sinclair's scorching contrast between this state of affairs and the simplicity of the Carpenter of Nazareth was probably more persuasive than cogent, but it made a deep impression upon me.

The fact is that the Episcopal Church's concern with social problems and its ability to stimulate in a surprisingly large number of members a fairly liberal, not to say radical, point of view about social and political affairs, is at least as important a part of its tradition as its reputation for attracting the privileged and well-born. The Church of England, for example, from which the Episcopal Church stems, has always conceived itself as responsible for the moral and spiritual welfare of the whole body of English society. A history of constructive proposals for social reform can be traced from the sermons of Hugh Latimer, one of the Reformation bishops, martyred under Queen Mary, through Archbishop Laud, to William Wilberforce and the "Clapham Sect" to the activities of nineteenth-century Broad Churchmen like Charles Kingsley and Frederick Denison Maurice and such Anglo-Catholic social thinkers as Charles Gore or V. A. Demant. A Church which could produce, for example, a Charles Kingsley who, on April 10, 1848, addressed a challenging message to the great Chartist gathering then being held in London, a message which was entitled "Working Men of England!" and was signed "A Working Parson," is obviously no Church to parrot the social prejudices only of the rich and mighty.

From the point of view of our American prejudice in favor of a separation of Church and State, it may be difficult to appreciate the advantages in social outlook which can conceivably result from an established ecclesiastical body. Whatever disadvantages establishment may have, it does not create a subservient or complacent Christian Church; at least it has not done so in the case of the Church of England. What it does produce is a sense of identification with the problems and issues which confront the national society, with a full acceptance of all the responsibilities that involvement in such questions carries with it. The sectarian ideal of the relationship of Christianity to society—an ideal which has been very influential in shaping Protestant social thought in America, for example—tends to think of the Church as an other-worldly society, sharply separated in its habits and thinking from the national society around it. Its primary obligation is to save people out of the national society rather than to save them *within* it. Its social message is often cast in a form of a scolding rebuke directed toward rather clearly defined worldly practices such as smoking, drinking, theatre-going, etc. The Church of England, of course, knew something of this spirit in the Evangelical Movement, especially as it arose under the influence of John Wesley and his colleagues in the late 18th century. By and large, however, Anglicanism has taken a much broader view of its social responsibilities than that and has been willing to accept the legitimacy of the world and its ways, seeking only within them to achieve higher levels of justice, freedom and mutuality.

A Church which seems by its moral teaching and social message to equate drinking a martini with suppressing the right of workmen to organize a labor union would appear to be in danger of confusing "tithing mint, anise and cummin" with "the weightier matters of the law." It has

been painful to one who believes in the possibilities of
united Protestant witness to observe how many times the
only social program about which Protestant ministers and
church leaders get really excited is the banning of beer
advertising on billboards when a whole host of injustices
and social evils in the community clamor for rebuke and
reform. The Episcopal Church is often regarded as being
hopelessly worldly in its outlook. No Episcopalian can
afford to dismiss this charge without seriously thinking
about it, but to equate worldliness with an acceptance of
harmless social habits and the identification of social
wickedness with such habits will always seem to an Episcopalian to involve the equal danger of moralism, censorious-
ness and an asceticism that comes perilously close to deny-
ing the goodness of God's creation.

   In the tumultuous social and political controversies of
the 1930's I was looking for a Church which took the social
problems of mankind with utter seriousness. In many ways
the Episcopal Church filled the bill. Like many other young
people of the time, I was deeply impressed with the economic and ethical persuasiveness of socialism. Somewhat
to my surprise, I found a respectable tradition of long
standing within Anglicanism which was willing to call
itself "Christian Socialism." The movement in the Church
of England which bore this name derived chiefly from the
labors of the famous Frederick Denison Maurice, but it
was carried on and had a more sustained impact upon
Church thinking through the work of several Anglo-
Catholics, principally Bishop Charles Gore and Canon
Henry Scott Holland. Their general conviction was
summed up in these words of Gore: "They were all at one

in feeling that the principles and life and spirit of Jesus
Christ had very much to do with the social question, and
would be found on serious investigation to have both an
illuminating power to be brought to bear on the relation of
man to man and an explosive force in the struggle against
injustice and the exploiting of the weak, which could not
be equalled anywhere else." * This point of view had great
influence and was given frequent expression in the Episcopal Church, especially between 1910 and 1940. Bishops'
pastoral letters and the minutes of many diocesan and
general conventions during that period reflect the Church's
intention to speak critically and constructively about the
conditions of man's social life. During my college and
seminary days the Church League for Industrial Democracy was actively at work, influencing large numbers of
younger clergy especially and occupying an important,
even if unofficial, part in the program of every General
Convention. In 1940, for example, Bishop Edward L.
Parsons of California explained the attitude of the CLID,
as it was known, to a reporter in the following words:
"What is wrong is the social order which expresses . . . the
selfishness and blindness of the human heart; a social order
which makes most Christians deny daily the essential meaning of their faith; a social order which puts the emphasis upon wealth and power, and consecrates the sin of
avarice." **

During my seminary days I attended several national
CLID conferences, at one of which I heard for the first

* Quoted in Fletcher, Jos. F., and Miller, Spencer: *The Church and
Industry*. 1930. Longmans, Green & Co. Page 20.
** *Kansas City Times,* Thursday, October 10, 1940, Page 5.

time an address by Reinhold Niebuhr. For many reasons
the forms in which these social interests expressed themselves before the Second World War have now very sub-
stantially changed. Perhaps one of the most important
reasons was the disillusionment that many of us felt over
Soviet Russia after the purge trials of 1937. Indeed, I think
it is fair to say the almost complete collapse of the CLID,
or as it later came to be named, the Episcopal League for
Social Action, can be traced to the differences between
those who felt this disillusionment sharply and others who
still felt that the Soviet experiment was a hopeful one and
deserved support in many of its aspects. Then, too, the
post-war world—in America, at least—has not produced an
atmosphere in which radical social reform has had much
popularity. The achievements of the New Deal have
seemed to many people to have resolved the most urgent
problems of social justice, and very few are in the mood for
new or continued crusades.

Only in the field of race relationships is a burning social
question still before the nation. Again there are many
evidences that the Episcopal Church is giving some brave
and constructive leadership in the facing of this issue. The
abolition in our Southern dioceses of separate Negro
congregations, and the racial integration of a surprising
number of diocesan-wide church activities, even in the
deep South, are encouraging signs of progress. The present
crisis in the South has proved the high quality of Negro
ministers, and those of the Episcopal Church are no exception. A white clergyman in the South complained to me
recently—but I took his complaint to be in reality a significant tribute to the dedication and ability of our Negro

priests there—that many of the Negro ministers are spending more time building up the National Association for
the Advancement of Colored People than they are in
building up the Episcopal Church. Such a criticism, even
if it is justified, misses the point that God is as much concerned with the way we treat our brethren of different races
as He is in much of the welter of church activity that too
often preoccupies the life of a parish clergyman.

The present importance of the question of racial integration points up one advantage which belongs to any Christion Church which, like the Episcopal Church, lays great
emphasis upon the Sacraments and the reality of the
Body of Christ as expressed in the worshipping fellowship
of the Church. Perhaps more easily than in churches which
stress the initiative and responsibility of the individual in
establishing his relationship to God, the Episcopal Church
even in the deep South has had a degree of integration in
worship and especially at the Holy Communion which is
characteristic of few other Churches, with the notable
exception of the Roman Catholic. Admittedly this degree
of fellowship is not enough, and one must confess that although Negroes and whites may often feed together upon
the Body and Blood of our Lord Jesus Christ, they do not
often enough reflect this basic unity in eating together at
a parish dinner or at a tea given by the women's organization. The early Anglo-Catholic Christian Socialists insisted
that in the sacramental character of the Christian Church
lay one of the most dynamic motivations for greater fellowship among men of all classes and races and nations. To the
extent that the Episcopal Church is a sacramental Church,
stressing equally the importance of the new relationship

to God which is made possible in Christ and the new relationship which is similarly made possible between a man
and his brother, it has always seemed to me to have a special
opportunity to demonstrate the social imperative of the
Christian faith. I well remember how in my days of enthusiasm for the New Deal I was impressed by the ways in
which Episcopalians like Frances Perkins and Henry Wal-
lace so obviously drew the inspiration for their political
and social attitudes and policies from their sacramental life.

It would be very misleading to suggest, however, that
all Episcopalians will read these last few paragraphs with
unmixed enthusiasm. The Episcopal Church has at least its
quota of social conservatives and even of social reaction-
aries. As I have grown older I have become somewhat more
realistic about the possibilities of using the Church as a
kind of advance guard in social and political thinking.
Too often the stirring resolutions which used to warm my
heart in my student days were not really representative of
the thinking of the average Churchman. I have become
somewhat more suspicious of the maneuvers of well-mean-
ing clergy and sometimes laity who seek to carry through
some convention or church meeting resolutions on social
and political matters which represent in reality the convictions of only a fraction of those in attendance. For all
that I have said about the tradition of social leadership
which exists in the Anglican Communion and in the Episcopal Church, I still suspect that my own political thinking
would be far to the left of that which would be revealed in
a real Gallup poll of Episcopalian opinion! Sometimes the
contrast is painful and shocking, and if I had retained only
my naive faith as a college senior that the Episcopal Church

was chiefly important as a rallying point for advanced social and political thinking, I should have abandoned that church some time ago. Like many other Americans of my generation, however, I have come to have a new respect for the contributions of the genuine Conservative, and I rejoice that both Conservative and Liberal versions of a Christian's political and social responsibility can exist together in the Episcopal Church with opportunities of confronting each other in study and thought, in worship and discussion. Once again the tradition of pulpit freedom, for example, has new significance for me and seems more than ever to be one of the strong points of the Episcopal Church. My own inclination would be to put more hope in the development of voluntary groups for advanced social and political thinking along Christian lines rather than in official resolutions by conferences and conventions. The declining influence of the Episcopal League for Social Action is, therefore, an even more lamentable loss. Perhaps a widespread recovery of concern for social transformation will have to take place within our society before this aspect of the Church's life will come once more into its own. I am content that an impressive tradition exists within Anglicanism and lives on today in the prophetic speaking and thinking of many of our bishops, clergy and leading laymen.

The social responsibility of a Christian is not exhausted, of course, in projects and hopes for the reformation of social institutions and political organizations. Like many other Christian bodies, the Episcopal Church has also taken a leading role in many American communities in sponsoring and encouraging a whole host of agencies which

seek to minister to men and women and children in special
cases of emergency and need. Hospitals, institutions for
child care, homes for aged people, services to underprivileged people and neighborhoods through programs of
recreation and fellowship, a ministry to indigent people
needing counsel and financial help and to inmates of
public institutions of care and correction—in all of these
ways the Episcopal Church has established a notable record
for good works and for neighborly service that is a source
of pride and humble gratitude to any one of her members.
It is interesting that perhaps more than most other
Protestant groups the Episcopal Church has given special
attention to the ministry in public institutions, especially
jails, penitentiaries, mental institutions, poor farms, re-
formatories, etc. This specialization reflects what I might
call the genius for pastoral care which I think is one of
the distinctive marks of Anglicanism. Perhaps again because of its sacramental character, the Episcopal Church
seems to rely less than other Protestant bodies on sermons
and exhortations. Perhaps it is the impersonality and
democracy of a service like the Holy Communion that
makes it so eloquent of divine forgiveness and human acceptance when it is celebrated in a penitentiary or an institution for psychiatric care. Someone has pointed out that
there are more Episcopalians than any other non-Roman
Catholic group of Christians in San Quentin Penitentiary!
I prefer to believe that this is evidence of the pastoral out-
reach of the Episcopal Church in such an institution rather
than an indication of an inherent tendency to delinquency
in people who worship by a prayer book!

The Episcopal Church has always welcomed the best

that the study of sociology and of the techniques and philosophy of social work can bring to the task of ministering to the suffering, the friendless and the needy. A department of the National Council of the Episcopal Church is entitled "The Department of Christian Social Relations" and one of its tasks is to urge the highest standards of social work upon Church-related institutions. This task is never wholly accomplished, of course, but its place at the heart of the Episcopal Church's national organization is a testimony to the seriousness with which it is taken.

The America of my college days has greatly changed and my earlier criteria of what constituted a prophetic and socially concerned Church have changed too. Nevertheless, I still believe that few other religious bodies can match the wisdom and the breadth and the understanding with which the Episcopal Church conceives and tackles its task of serving the human family and lifting it to higher levels of justice and mutuality. This is one of the reasons I am an Episcopalian.

EIGHT

"IN UNITY AND GODLY LOVE"

ALTHOUGH I became an Episcopalian after having spent the major part of my childhood in more or less close contact with other Church traditions, I believe I have somehow avoided the temptation which besets so many converts, namely, to minimize the importance and validity of other Christian bodies. Especially in the American scene, where the Episcopal Church is often a very small minority of the total religiously committed population, it has always seemed to me pompous and foolish—as well as profoundly unchristian—to assume that the only authentic Christian experience was to be found in the Episcopal Church and that the endless praises of Heaven were probably being conducted according to the Prayer Book of 1549! This attitude, which is embarrassingly widespread, derives in part, I think, from the fact that the Episcopal Church is made up so largely of people who have come into it from other religious traditions and have done so as a matter of conscience

and distinct preference. Perhaps it is a result of the linger-
ing sense of the privileges and responsibilities of an established church. I cannot imagine quite how I escaped falling
into something of this attitude myself, since I find that I
am often tempted beyond my strength to be dogmatic and
to absolutize my preferences and tastes.

Part of the credit ought to be given to a unique inter-
faith organization in Southern California to which I was
introduced in my college years. It is the University Religious Conference, a cooperative undertaking supported by
the outstanding religious leadership of the Southern California community, including the Roman Catholic Archbishop, the Episcopal Bishop, one of the leading Jewish
Rabbis, and almost every important religious official in
the area. Because of its representative character, the University Religious Conference was never tempted to suggest
that important differences of creedal viewpoint could be
waived aside as insignificant. Its motto was: "We agree to
disagree agreeably." In the building provided by this
unique and exciting organization the religious activities
at the University of California at Los Angeles, barred by
state law from using the campus facilities themselves, took
place. In my senior year in college I lived and worked in
this building, and on the basis of my services as dish-
washer, waiter and occasionally assistant to the cook, I can
claim a first-hand knowledge of inter-faith affairs, especially
as seen from the perspective of dietary peculiarities!

In such a setting, it was inevitable that personal friend-
ships would spring up across religious lines, and that occasional instances of official cooperation would take place.
In later years I often spoke as the representative of the

Protestant tradition along with Roman Catholic and
Jewish friends on the familiar "trialogue" pattern, a responsibility which helped to focus areas both of agreement
and disagreement among the major religious traditions as
well as within the Protestant family of communions and
denominations. Two years at the Yale Divinity School, an
interdenominational graduate school of theology, helped
to broaden my knowledge and interest in other religious
groups as well as to reinforce my own convictions and
preferences with respect to Anglicanism. Like many other
working clergymen, I have participated always in ministerial associations and church federations, a responsibility
which I have always thought a clergyman owes some time
to, even if the experience is not always very rewarding.
All of this background is presently useful as I seek to
administer the religious program of a great university,
where every conceivable religious position, not only of
the American variety but from all over the world, is
represented.

The Episcopal Church has an important role to play, in
the first place, in the development of the characteristically
American inter-faith movement. I know of no other single
Church which is able to understand so fully the distinctive
outlooks both of Protestantism and of Roman Catholicism
as is the Episcopal Church. What is more, its deep reliance
upon the Bible, its wide use of the Psalms in its worship
and its specification for both an Old Testament and a New
Testament Lesson in its Daily Offices, gives it a natural
affinity with and understanding of Judaism. Elizabethan
Anglicanism has bequeathed a curious kind of irenic in-
clusiveness to its daughter Churches. This does not mean,

of course, that theological orthodoxy is taken lightly. We shall see presently that the very opposite is the case. There is, however, an almost indefinable sense of the proprieties of inter-faith contact which has its roots, I believe, in the relationships to Roman Catholicism and Judaism which have just been referred to. If the inter-faith movement in America is to achieve its maximum potentialities, it must move from the realm of mere polite gestures to genuine theological discussion and encounter. I believe that the Anglican tradition has a very special contribution to make to this kind of undertaking.

I have been increasingly aware that the Episcopal Church has what seems to me an enormous advantage in inter-denominational activities within non-Roman Christianity. In the first place, the problem of the character and life of the Church is considered in Anglicanism to be a matter of the deepest importance. In contrast to certain other Protestant churches of a more sectarian tradition, Anglicanism has always insisted that the life of the Church and her sacraments must be thought of as necessary "means of grace." Church life is not an elective which a Christian may take on out of a sense of duty and responsibility but may omit without serious damage to his faith. The fact is he cannot really be a Christian apart from involvement in the community of believers.

Anglicanism, furthermore, has always had a lively interest in the unity of the Church. Of course, no Christian who takes the Bible seriously can overlook the importance of maintaining a visible witness in a united Christian fellowship to the reconciling power of the love of God in Christ. "That they may be one" was not only a pious aspiration of our Lord's but was His description of one of the Church's essential characteristics. One of the advantages of the background of an established church is that it gives seriousness and urgency to the problem of expressing in one broad ecclesiastical framework as inclusive a sampling of the varieties of Christian attitude and discipleship as possible. From the very beginnings of the Reformation, Anglican leaders exhibited the greatest concern for the cause of Christian unity. Church historians tell us that Archbishop Cranmer, for example, urged in vain that some of the continental leaders, chiefly Melancthon, draw together a representative group of continental Protestant leaders for conference and consultation with the Anglicans in order to secure a unification of the Reformation forces. Richard Hooker, in his *Laws of Ecclesiastical Polity,* urges that differences of theological emphasis, for example, ought not to be encouraged among the several national Churches that shared in the Reformation movement, but ought to be reserved for resolution at a broadly representative conference that he hopes will be called before too long. The Reformation churches, according to Hooker, would have been wise to have adopted their distinctive positions and established their ministry and polity "in more wary and suspense manner, as being to stand in force until God should give the opportunity of some general conference what might be best for every of them afterward to do." (*Laws of Ecclesiastical Polity,* Preface, II, 2.)

It was, therefore, perhaps with some inevitability that the Episcopal Church took a leading role in the initiation of what has now come to be called the Ecumenical Movement. Indeed no other religious body except the Disciples

of Christ can claim to have done more. Charles Henry
Brent, Bishop of the Philippine Islands and later of Western New York, introduced at the General Convention of
1910 at Cincinnati the proposal which led to the great
World Conferences on Faith and Order and later on Life
and Work and which has now brought about the establishment of the World Council of Churches. Characteristically,
Bishop Brent's proposal did not suggest cavalier dismissal
of theological and ecclesiastical differences but proposed
only that by means of conference and consultation the real
nature of these differences might be investigated and the
areas of agreement and disagreement clearly delineated.
American Protestantism is often guilty of thinking of
Christian unity in terms of abandoning all our old "prejudices" and achieving some mechanical amalgamation which
is to be equated with the Holy Catholic Church of the
ages. Anglicanism takes the Church and its faith too seriously for this kind of treatment. Episcopalians cannot be
expected, therefore, to enter into what are essentially premature attempts to achieve Christian reunion by fiat.
It is sometimes claimed that a self-styled "inter-denominational" church has achieved the ecumenical ideal. It is not
unknown that some such churches even boast of the fact
that they include Episcopalians in their membership. This,
of course, is in fact impossible. No Episcopalian in good
standing will ever abandon the communion of his own
Church to join one of the amalgamated organizations.
Obviously, far from being ecumenical, such so-called inter-
denominational churches really deny the validity of the
whole process which has been going on now for more than
a quarter of a century and which is generally known as

the Ecumenical Movement. The long conversations on Faith and Order, for example, which have been going between Anglicans, Lutherans, Presbyterians, Eastern Orthodox, and many other non-Roman Catholic bodies for more than a quarter of a century, assume that theological consensus, at least on major issues, must precede ecclesiastical amalgamation. For many American Protestants this seems too slow and burdensome a line of action and with characteristic American impatience they have decided to solve the problem forthwith. At the risk of being labelled as non-cooperative, Episcopalians generally avoid such precipitant projects.

A similar explanation needs to be made with respect to the practice of what is usually called "closed communion" in the Episcopal Church. It is true that not all Episcopalians are agreed about this practice and that vigorous debate has raged for some time about the meaning of the rubric in the Prayer Book upon which the practice is generally based. The rubric, which comes at the end of the Confirmation Service, says that "there shall none be admitted to the Holy Communion, until such time as he be confirmed, or be ready and desirous to be confirmed." Advocates of the practice of "open communion" urge that this rubric, since it was written and appeared in English canon law before the Reformation, cannot have been directed toward the problem of separated Christian Churches but rather toward the problem of the neglect of Confirmation by pre-Reformation English Churchmen and to make clear that children are not to be admitted to Communion until they have reached the age of "discretion" and have been trained and presented for Confirmation. I have always

felt some of the force of this argument, but I have never
felt free to extend sweeping and general invitations to the
Communion—as is often done—to "anyone who wants to
come" or "any professed Christians" or "to any baptized
persons." For if an individual clergyman by an announce-
ment from the chancel steps can achieve inter-communion,
then what is all the excitement about in the lengthy discussions which go on through the Ecumenical Movement?
Is there any kind of unity more important than unity in
the sacrament of the Holy Communion? If this has already
been achieved or can be achieved by individual clergymen
acting on their own initiative, then it would seem to me
that the cause of Christian reunion has already been completely successful in attaining its objectives. To those who
object that it is scandalous and shocking to separate Christians at the Table of the Lord, the only reply is that it is
indeed but that this separation is only a symbol of the real
separation that exists between "those who profess and call
themselves Christians." That is the real scandal after all.

Not all that calls itself ecumenical has necessarily any
affinity to the world movement that usually goes by this
name. Much cooperative American Protestant activity,
especially on the local level, is on a very shallow and
superficial basis. I have been as active as anyone else in
the field of cooperative Protestantism, and have served as
president of a great metropolitan church federation and
in another instance led in the formation of a community
council of churches. I must confess that I have often been
in despair, however, at the unwillingness of most American
Protestants to discuss the significant theological differences
which separate them or to come to any kind of profound

agreement about the meaning of the Christian faith and its
relationship to community life. It is usually assumed that
such agreement exists, but at any moment a critical issue
may arise which makes it perfectly evident how unwarranted this assumption is. If all that united Protestantism
can do is to deal with liquor, gambling and any signs of
aggressiveness on the part of Roman Catholics, then it
would be better if American Protestantism gave up its
cooperative witness as soon as possible! The more theologically and ecclesiastically minded denominations, however, are sometimes to blame for the state of affairs that
exists within cooperative Protestantism, because they absent themselves from meetings and only privately criticize
and deride the results. One of the reasons I am an Episcopalian is because I believe the Episcopal Church with its
broad theological platform, consisting of the great essentials
of the Christian faith, and its witness by its apostolic
ministry to the continuity of the Christian tradition down
through the centuries, has an important contribution to
make to ecumenical Christianity.

One of the reasons, however, why I am often ashamed
of being an Episcopalian is that with a quite indefensible
air of superiority so many Episcopalians, both clerical and
lay, hold themselves aloof from cooperative Protestant
activities, not because of theological convictions but because of social and ecclesiastical snobbishness. The leadership given to the Ecumenical Movement by such undeniably orthodox Anglican leaders as Bishop Charles Brent or
Archbishop William Temple invalidates the suggestion
that such participation involves any lessening of loyalty to
Anglicanism itself. The breadth of such a document, for

example, as the "Letter to All Christian People" from the
Lambeth Conference of 1920 ought to reassure and challenge the cautious and conservative among us. "We believe
that God wills fellowship . . . we believe that it is God's
purpose to manifest this fellowship . . . in an outward,
visible and united society, holding one faith, having its
own recognized officers, using God's given means of grace,
and inspiring all its members to the world-wide service of
the Kingdom of God. This is what we mean by the Catholic
Church . . . This united fellowship is not visible in the
world today . . . The vision which rises before us is that of
a Church genuinely Catholic, loyal to all Truth, and
gathering into its fellowship all who profess and call themselves Christians . . . May we not reasonably claim that the
Episcopate is one means of providing . . . a ministry acknowledged by every part of the Church? . . . It is not that
we call in question for a moment the spiritual reality of
the ministries of those Communions who do not possess the
Episcopate. On the contrary, we thankfully acknowledge
that these ministries have been manifestly blessed and
owned by the Holy Spirit as effective means of grace."

To any Christian who is drawn to the Episcopal Church
but feels that its slow and cautious approach to the question of Christian reunion may be hindering the advancement of that important purpose, there is reassurance to be
found in the experiment of the Church of South India.
Although world Anglicanism is approaching that Church
in a very cautious and gingerly way, it seems safe to
predict that the advances that have been made in mutual understanding and toward full inter-communion will
be crowned with success before too many decades have

passed. In the meantime, the lesson of the Church of South India is instructive. The distinctive things for which Anglicanism stands—the spiritual authority of the bishop as the shepherd and teacher of the flock of Christ, and an indigenous liturgy based upon the proportion of faith as it is demonstrated in the historic creeds and the traditional sacraments of the Baptism and the Holy Communion—have been enthusiastically received and claimed by the non-Anglicans who have entered into the United Church. This is so much the case that proposed discussions for incorporating Lutheran bodies into the United Church have had to face the difficulty that the Church of South India will now no longer treat the Episcopate as a subject for discussion, since it has come to regard it as an essential for its life. It is possible that many non-Episcopalians are only held back from a recognition of the validity of the episcopal form of government and the advantages of a liturgy by the exclusive claims and the air of superiority with which these treasures are treated by Anglicans themselves! Because it seems to me that the Anglican Communion has discovered an important secret of Christian unity and an important clue to the path along which Christian reunion will be achieved, I rejoice in my membership in that Communion and only pray that it may more and more make its full contribution to the achievement of the purpose of the great Shepherd and Bishop of our souls "that they all may be one."

NINE

"THROUGHOUT ALL THE WORLD"

TO BE AN Episcopalian, of course, involves one at once in membership in an extraordinarily close-knit, worldwide fellowship known as the Anglican Communion. It used to be said that "the sun never sets on the British Empire," and for this reason it is still true today that the sun never sets on the Anglican Communion, which has sprung up wherever English-speaking people have gone. In every continent of the world, drawn from every major racial group, Anglicanism represents an important and distinctive tradition within the great worldwide Christian Church. It embraces more than 300 dioceses and includes about 40 million baptized members.

The following are the major autonomous National Churches that make up this far-flung Christian tradition: The Church of England; the Episcopal Church in Scotland; the Church of Ireland; the Church of Wales; the Protestant Episcopal Church in the United States of

America; the Holy Catholic Church of China; the Holy
Catholic Church of Japan; the Anglican Church of Can-
ada; the Church of the Province of the West Indies;
the Church of India, Pakistan, Burma and Ceylon; the
Church of the Province of Central Africa; the Church of
the Province of South Africa; the Church of the Province
of West Africa; the Church of England in Australia and
Tasmania; the Church of the Province of New Zealand.
In addition to these great National Churches, there are
19 separated dioceses established under the authority of
the Archbishop of Canterbury but not considered as in-
tegral parts of any of the other autonomous national
churches.

This vast and variegated company of Christians is held
together not by any legal structure nor official ecclesiastical
connections but by its loyalty to the essential ideals of
the English Reformation, namely, episcopal government
by apostolic succession, liturgical worship, the Bible interpreted by the Creeds and tradition as the source of
doctrine. Since the oldest see in the Anglican Communion
is that of Canterbury, the Archbishop is regarded as
primus inter pares (first among equals) in respect and ven-
eration. The present Archbishop by his world travels has
contributed impressively to the growing sense of Anglican
unity around the world and helped to symbolize and express the Anglican ideal of reformed Catholic Christianity.

From the day of Pentecost, it has been one of the glories
of the Christian Church that it is able to transcend differences of nationality, language and culture, and to initiate
its members into a world community. An Episcopalian is
made vividly aware of the reality of this fact by the con-

stant recollection of his membership in the Anglican
Communion. What a warming sense of acceptance and
fellowship there is in the discovery, for example, thousands
of miles from home in Westminster Abbey, St. George's
Cathedral in Jerusalem, or a parish church in New Zealand of familiar prayers, canticles, and a pattern of ordered
worship and sacramental life which is one's own familiar
spiritual nourishment! The contributions of the English-
speaking peoples of the world continue to grow in range
and importance. The Anglican Communion is the chief
religious expression of the life of English-speaking people,
and its Book of Common Prayer will be in use as a matter
of course wherever the English tongue is spoken. Of course,
in some parts of the Anglican Communion the liturgy has
been translated into other native tongues on the original
principle that the services should always be "in a language
understanded of the people." But even in such places, for
one who does not understand the native language, there is
still a real sense of familiarity in the age-old patterns of
liturgical and sacramental worship and life.

The history of the development of this great Christian
tradition has been traced by some unthinking or unfriendly
critics to Henry VIII. Since it seems inevitable that a
discussion of this gentleman, his marital tastes and practices and his ecclesiastical accomplishments, arises whenever Anglicanism is discussed, perhaps this is a place in
this little book for a brief exercise in Church history!
All Anglicans resent the crediting of Henry VIII with the
foundation of their Communion, not only because it is
thoroughly bad history but because it reflects a special
definition of the Catholic Church which Anglicanism has

always denied. Ever since William the Conqueror, the Church of England had been in more or less continuous controversy with the Bishop of Rome, to whom Roman Catholics give the title of Pope. This controversy found expression in laws, for example, which denied the right of the Papacy to nominate bishops in England and which forbade appeals from English church courts to any ecclesiastical court outside of the kingdom. Admittedly this legislation, which was passed in the middle of the 14th century, had become a dead letter, but it indicates the ambition for autonomy and freedom which had animated the English Church long before Henry VIII's time. No one I have ever met would want to defend this monarch's marital record, although it must be confessed that in the case which brought about the assertion of the Church of England's independence of Rome, he had an extraordinarily good point in his favor. The truth was that his marriage to Catherine of Aragon had been undertaken in violation of church law with the special permission of the Pope himself. Henry doubted—admittedly somewhat later when he had found what seemed to him a more suitable bride—the legality of the former Pope's action. His doubts, incidentally, were supported by the leading theological scholars and canon lawyers of his day. The important point is that when he declared the Church of England to be essentially autonomous and independent from the jurisdiction of the Pope he did nothing to alter its essential character nor even to disturb the ordinary course of its life. Most of the bishops continued to hold their sees, most of the clergy retained their benfices and parish responsibilities, most of the people worshipped on the Sunday after

Parliament had declared Henry VIII to be the supreme head of the Church of England in very much the same way that they worshipped the Sunday before.

To a Roman Catholic, of course, this change was all-important, since communion with the Bishop of Rome is, on their theory of the Church, an absolute necessity. Consequently a Roman Catholic must insist that everything changed when Parliament made its declaration of royal supremacy. A whole new ecclesiastical organization was begun, on the Roman Catholic theory, by that action, but, of course, even if the Roman Catholic theory is granted, the truth is that under Queen Mary the whole national Church was once again obliged to make its submission to the Roman authority, and Henry's work was completely undone. So even Roman Catholics ought to argue that Elizabeth I started the Anglican Communion. Anglicans themselves, obviously, would insist that all that occurred either under Henry, his son Edward VI, or under Elizabeth I, was that the Church underwent a period of reformation, thoroughgoing and drawing its inspiration both from the continental Protestant Reformation and from the tradition of Renaissance Humanism. The distinguishing marks of the communion which received such important influences from these events is the burden of many chapters of this little book. We proudly claim the tradition of English-speaking Christianity. From St. Patrick through the heroic names of Anselm, Thomas Cranmer, William Laud, John Wesley, John Henry Newman, and a whole host of contemporary Anglican leaders, the Anglican Communion has received a rich and goodly heritage, despite the fact that some of these ancestors have separated themselves finally from her tradition. Into this proud heritage, every Episcopalian enters by virtue of his Baptism and Confirmation. The marks of these heroes and many other lesser known saints of the past are found in her Prayer Book, Hymnal and body of Canon Law. Not as a dead curiosity from the past but as a living and present spiritual resource, the Anglican tradition is inevitably one of the glories of being an Episcopalian.

The spread of Anglican influence, of course, still goes on. With vigor and enthusiasm, the Protestant Episcopal Church in America, for example, carries on a widespread missionary activity. With the closing of China as a missionary field after the Communists came to power there, the American Episcopal Church has lost one of its traditionally important centers of missionary activity. New areas of strategic importance have, however, opened up in recent years. One of the most exciting is in the new nation of the Philippines. A small but impressive missionary activity began there with the American occupation of the Islands after the Spanish-American War. This activity, in deference to already established Christian work, was limited to American citizens and to hitherto unevangelized mountain tribes. However, in recent years the Episcopal Church has suddenly moved into a position of great prominence through its close and fraternal relationships with the Philippine Independent Church, one of the major non-Roman Catholic bodies in the Islands. The American Episcopal Church bestowed the apostolic succession upon the Bishops of the Philippine Independent Church in a history-making Service of Consecration held in 1950. The Episcopal Seminary in the Philippines is now training a large number of the new clergy of the Philippine Independent Church, and it is confidently expected that closer and closer relationships will develop between the two. Another major area of recent missionary activity has been Central and South America. From the Panama Canal Zone as a center, work has spread into Colombia and Venezuela and up into Nicaragua, Costa Rica and Honduras. Equally dramatic developments have taken place in Brazil, where an original small diocese has blossomed into three dioceses with vigorous activity and growth.

The supervision and support of the missionary enterprise of the Episcopal Church centers in a greystone building at 281 Fourth Avenue in New York City. Since one of the traditional roles of the bishop has been the extension of the Church within the boundaries of his jurisdiction, the missionary work of the Episcopal Church centers around her missionary bishops. Some of them have been great and famous Christian heroes, such as Samuel Schereschewsky, the great scholar-bishop of China, or Peter Trimble Rowe, the pioneer Bishop of Alaska. It is the responsibility of a missionary bishop, with the support of a budget provided him in part by the national Church and in part from his own people, to shepherd the Episcopalians within his district and to seek out opportunities to plant the Church in new places and to extend the boundaries and effectiveness of the Episcopal Church's influence. In the Caribbean, in Liberia, in Brazil, in Alaska, in Honolulu, in the Philippine Islands, and in many sparsely settled areas of the Far West, the Episcopal Church is symbolized by one of the successors of the Apostles, and he can claim that succession not only by reason of the laying on of hands but by reason of the brave and adventuresome apostolic task which he daily undertakes.

Early in its career the American Episcopal Church made an important decision. In doing so, she turned her back on a venerable tradition of the Church of England which encouraged the foundation of missionary societies. To the Society for the Propagation of the Gospel the American colonies owed the first establishment of the Anglican Communion in this country. Later the Church Missionary Society carried the Christian gospel into many remote and difficult places. The American Episcopal Church decided to stake its future on a bolder idea. That was that the whole Church must consider itself a missionary society. The proclamation of the Gospel and the extension of its saving and transforming influence in the lives of men is not an elective which a few pious members of the Church may choose as a special form of spiritual exercise. It is the inevitable responsibility of every baptized person. This identification of the work of missions with the total structure of the Church has proved to be an inspired decision. It has kept the missionary activity of the Church responsive to the will and purpose of the total membership and has virtually ruled out the possibility of competitive missionary activities representing the various points of view within the Church. Admittedly this development was very late in coming, due to the preoccupation of the early Episcopalians after the Revolutionary War with the problems of reorganization and the even more formidable task of commending a form of Christianity which had been associated with England. That was a serious handicap in the newly independent country that was often impatient of reminders of its former colonial status.

Not until 1833 did the Episcopal Church begin to take its missionary responsibilities with real seriousness. As a result its spread in the United States itself was spotty and erratic. An examination of church statistics reveals that the Church is numerically weakest in the sections of the country that were settled before 1835 but encouragingly stronger in parts of the country settled after that time. The Episcopal Church was all too late in reaching Kentucky, Indiana or Missouri, but it arrived with the pioneers in the Rocky Mountain states and on the Pacific slope. It is a nation-wide Church, and there is no important city in America where there is not a vigorous and thriving parish. A good start, a near collapse after the Revolution, a slow recovery, a surprising burst of activity in the last hundred years—this is a brief sketch of the missionary impulse of American Anglicanism. Many of us feel that it has yet to make its major impact upon American life, and that its days of greater influence lie ahead of it. With the decline of the British Empire, of course, the Anglican Communion has faced serious crises in many parts of the world. The rise of nationalistic feeling in Asia and, perhaps, now in Africa, accompanied by a rising self-consciousness of the traditional religions of Islam, Hinduism and Buddhism, pose great challenges for world-wide Anglicanism.

Fortunately the challenge is being confronted by a more closely united Anglican Communion than has ever been known before in history. Since the latter part of the 19th century the bishops of the Anglican Communion have been meeting about once every ten years in what has be-

come known as the Lambeth Conference, its title drawn
from the name of the Palace which is the London head-
quarters of the Archbishop of Canterbury. Originally
looked upon with some suspicion, the Conference has
emerged, despite its lack of official or legal character, as an
all-important influence in world Anglicanism. Its decisions
and pronouncements have been of enormous importance,
chiefly hitherto in the whole matter of Christian reunion.
However, it seems likely that in the decades ahead it may
be even more significant in world evangelism and the
strategy of the Anglican Communion in that enterprise.
In 1954 the first world-wide Anglican Congress was held in
Minneapolis, an experiment which drew together for consultation, lectures and common worship representatives
from the whole face of the earth wherever an Anglican
Church exists. The enthusiastic reports of that Conference
and the deepening sense of world-wide unity which resulted make it safe to prophesy that another such congress
will be held sometime in the near future.

So the Anglican Church has grown beyond the bounds
of the British Isles, has passed to America where it has
become thoroughly at home, and indeed has been carried
to the uttermost parts of the earth. To be an Episcopalian
is to have the stimulating sense of living in this ancient
and venerable tradition of British Christianity, now become indigenous on every continent and in an astonishing
variety of languages and cultures. "From the rising of the
sun even unto the going down of the same" Christ is worshipped and His Gospel preached and the life of the Apostolic Church continued in its essentials. Here is one of the
deepest satisfactions of being an Episcopalian.

TEN

"THAT HOLY FELLOWSHIP"

IT SEEMS rather late in this book to say something
so perfectly obvious, but one of the attractive things
about the Episcopal Church is the Episcopalian one gets
to know! To begin life in the Episcopal Church as a choir
boy may not be a typical introduction to an Episcopal congregation, for he is likely to be unduly flattered and made
over, especially by ladies of the congregation with a strong
maternal instinct. The fact is that I was figuratively—and
sometimes literally—embraced with unmistakable affection
when I first made my bow as an Episcopal choirboy. And
this may be the reason why I have never seen much justice
in the characterization of the typical Episcopal congregation as cold and distant and aloof. It must be admitted, of
course, that the Episcopal Church bears the marks of its
English background, and that one of these marks is a kind
of reserve and formality which can sometimes be mistaken
by the demonstrative American as coldness and hauteur.

143

But just as I have never really found the English unfriendly, so I have never believed that Episcopalians were
less generously supplied with the milk of human kindness
than other religious people. The tradition by which the
Church is reserved for worship, of course, precludes hearty
greetings and neighborly chatting within its walls. This is
not because Episcopalians believe that God is displeased
with neighborliness. It is rather a recognition of the fact
that one of the ways of expressing neighborliness is to
allow your neighbor to prepare himself for worship without the distractions of your effusive greetings or idle conversations with a friend several pews away. We have already
pointed out that one of the important ways in which the
Episcopal Church creates the mood of worship among its
people is by the custom of spending some time in prayer
in preparation for the beginning of the service. The spectacle of people coming quietly into the church, kneeling
down, saying their prayers, and then sitting quietly reading through the hymnal or Prayer Book suggests just as
important a truth about the Christian life as does the spectacle of hearty and cheerful greetings and conversation
among the assembling congregation.

In most parishes a stranger will find a quiet but genuine
welcome from the usher and, as he leaves the church, from
the clergyman and others of the congregation. In many
churches the cheerful custom of a coffee hour after the
service—a custom dubbed by a friend of mine "thirst after
righteousness"—has made its appearance and aids greatly
in creating an atmosphere of friendliness and welcome. It
is important, however, not to confuse ordinary congen-
iality with the supernatural unity and fellowship based

upon Christian love which is the distinctive mark of the Christian Church. Someone has pointed out that although we are obliged to love our neighbors nobody can possibly require that we like them! This is, perhaps, to overstate the point, but there is a kind of false heartiness and self-conscious fellowship which sometimes intrudes itself into a Christian congregation but which has as little as possible to do with the real bond of Christian love which unites a congregation made up of diversified temperaments and attitudes. Like all other churches, the Episcopal Church provides any number of opportunities for expressing fellowship, but it must be confessed that oftentimes such organizations are based more on similarity of social status, educational background and temperament than they are upon a deep understanding of what it means to be accepted and to accept others in Christ.

It has been my privilege to serve parishes which drew upon a very wide variety of people to make up its membership. In several cases we have included within one fellowship several millionaires as well as a great many manual laborers, small shopkeepers, school teachers and almost every variety of social background and occupation. At the center of such a variegated fellowship of people is, however, one central and saving relationship, expressed in the sacrament of the Holy Communion. In this parish of mine, for example, two of the people who frequently came to the early celebration of the Holy Communion on Sunday mornings were one of the leading bankers of the metropolitan area in which the church was located and a laundress from the local hospital. Frequently they knelt side by side at the altar rail, and I was struck once again by

the unique capacity of the Christian Church to establish
fellowship over all the natural barriers and divisions of
the human family. I don't suppose that, humanly speaking, those two communicants had much in common. Indeed, my guess is that it would have been extraordinarily
difficult to have them develop any kind of what the world
calls "fellowship" outside of their fellowship at the communion rail. They had very few, if any, interests in common and their backgrounds of education and temperament
would make it difficult to communicate whatever similarity of interests might really exist. Their presence together at the altar rail proclaimed, however, that they were
equally loved by God and equally used by Him for the
achievement of His purposes among men. As Mr. C. S.
Lewis has pointed out,* the original Biblical conception
of Christian fellowship is expressed by St. Paul in the
simile of the human body. Membership, says Mr. Lewis,
in a human body is not a matter of being one unit among
other similar units, all of them interchangeable one with
the other. On the contrary, the members of the human
body are unique and irreplaceable and cannot be inter-
changed. "The eye cannot say unto the hand, I have no
need of thee." Obviously, says St. Paul, not all parts of the
body are equal in what he calls "honor" nor "comeliness."
It ought not to require much observation of the Christian
Church as it is found in a typical congregation to substan-
tiate St. Paul's conclusions! The wholesale method by
which the Church reaches out and gathers to herself all
men who feel the need of her Gospel and her life means
that of necessity a very mixed bag will result. No other

* Cf. "Membership" in "The Weight of Glory."

institution in society, of course, attempts to do what the Church does in opening her doors wide to allow anyone to come in without any credentials whatever. The university with its office of admissions, the country club with its membership committee, the Daughters of the American Revolution with their careful scrutinizing of one's genealogy—all of these are typical of the ways in which the societies of the world create unity and mutuality. The Church attempts a more daring experiment. It not only invites everyone in who wants to come; it also proposes to create such a sense of mutuality and communion that the social organism that results must be compared to the family in intimacy and closeness.

At least as well as most other churches I know and a great deal more inclusively than many, the Episcopal Church seems to me to fulfil this ideal of a catholic and universal Church. Although I have no statistics to prove this, I have the impression, for example, that a larger percentage of college faculty people belong to the Episcopal Church than to any other single denomination or communion. On the other hand, the Episcopal Church has had great success in New York City, as well as in other places, in attracting newly arrived Puerto Ricans into its churches. I have the impression that the Episcopal Church has more than its quota of eccentrics in its membership! While I may just be reflecting the exasperation of a pastor who has had to deal with the troublesome problem of adjusting such people to the requirements of church life and fellowship, I am inclined to think that this reflects the objectivity of Anglican worship and the wide liberty that is permitted in expressing one's devotion. While I am sure that pastors

of other denominations and traditions will rush to defend
their reputation for eccentricity also, I am willing to leave
it this way, that the Episcopal Church has as wide a variety
of people within its membership as any other Christian
body on the face of the earth. Perhaps one of the reasons
why Episcopalians have gained the unenviable title of
"God's frozen people" is that in addition to the English
tradition of reserve in personal relationships, there is also
oftentimes wider disparity in an Episcopal congregation
of economic, educational and social status than exists in at
least many other Protestant churches.

Like any other body of American Christians, Episcopalians, of course, express their essential unity with one
another in a wide variety of organizations and societies.
Certainly the most impressive in terms of size and of the
effectiveness of its work is the Woman's Auxiliary to the
National Council. This is the one inclusive organization
of the women of the Episcopal Church which is intended
to unify and coordinate everything that is done by women
in the fields of study, worship, service and fellowship.
Their usefulness to the clergy and their services to the
parishes where they are established are beyond calcula-
tion. The imagination staggers at the number of dinners,
the miles of knitting, the assortment of rummage, the gal-
lons of tea and coffee, the electricity employed in pressing
and ironing, and all the other statistics that might be compiled about the contribution of the women of the Episcopal Church to its program and life. More important,
however, than this discipleship of Martha is the discipleship of Mary which the Woman's Auxiliary exemplifies. It
is the single most effective organization for adult education

in the Episcopal Church. Bible classes, study courses in missions, lectures on civic and community problems which challenge the Christian conscience—these and any number of other projects designed to help the Churchwoman understand more deeply her faith and her Church go to make up the educational record of this remarkable organization. One of the great thrills of my proximity to the New York Cathedral has been the opportunity to participate, for example, in the "School of Worship" sponsored annually by the Woman's Auxiliary of the Diocese of New York. Hundreds of women fill the choir and crossing of the Cathedral for the sessions of these schools. Great credit goes to the leaders of this organization in the past and the present who have held up this ideal of study and of worship as equal in significance to the more familiar—and perhaps more easily comprehended—tasks of service and fund raising.

No mention of the Woman's Auxiliary, however, would be complete without a reference to its superlative record of missionary giving as expressed through the United Thank Offering. The Offering has its origin in the familiar Christian experience of gratitude and thanksgiving. Through the work of a local branch of the Woman's Auxiliary every woman in the parish is urged to accept a "Blue Box," a familiar sight in the kitchen of many Episcopal women. Into this Blue Box go special offerings from time to time when one is moved to thank God for all His many mercies. Twice a year the contents of these boxes are presented at the altar of the parish church in connection with a celebration of the Holy Communion or at one of the other services.

The climax comes in the presentation of the total offering of the women of the Church for the past three years at the time of the Triennial General Convention. This service, which is a celebration of the Holy Communion presided over by the Presiding Bishop, who is assisted in the administration of the Communion by all the Missionary Bishops who are present at the Convention, is a thrilling experience, never to be forgotten by those who have taken part in it. From every diocese and missionary district of the Episcopal Church—from New York, California, Florida and all the other 48 States as well as from Alaska, Brazil, Liberia and many other distant parts of the world, come the representatives of the women of the Church with their great "sacrifice of praise and thanksgiving." As the Presiding Bishop lifts high the golden alms basin in which the offering is traditionally presented and the great assemblage of thousands of women join in the singing of the Doxology, one feels more deeply than ever before the goodness of God and the wonderful capacity for gratitude and thanksgiving which He creates in His children. In recent years the offering has risen till it now represents several millions of dollars, and the distribution of this gift to assist in the mission and program of the Church is one of the major business responsibilities of the triennial meeting of the women of the Church. For many years one of the major sources of funds for capital expansion in the mission fields, for example, has come from this gift of the women. One thrills to belong to a Church which can claim in such a dramatic way the loyalty and devotion of its women.

In the midst of our rhapsody, however, it may be sobering to recall one serious flaw in the life of the Episcopal

Church—at least, so it appears to me—and that is the continued refusal of the Church to claim the services of its women in its regular organs and channels of church government. One must report with shame and regret that although women have made their way into the Congress of the United States and have served there with conspicuous distinction, they are still officially regarded as second-class citizens by the General Convention of the Episcopal Church. Obviously not all Episcopalians will agree with me, for ever since 1949 the General Convention has consistently turned down efforts to permit dioceses and missionary districts to send women as lay delegates to the Convention. As one who has had to suffer through many interminable debates, I must say that in my opinion there seems to be no logic whatever in this denial. Arguments that the women don't want this responsibility, that their eligibility might tempt the men of the Church to abdicate the field (an insult to the laymen of the Church which I should think they ought to be the first to resent), that women are temperamentally unsuited for the rough give-and-take of convention debates (a contention amply disproved by the experience of the United States Senate—and one assumes that General Convention seldom descends to lower depths of roughness than that august body!)—all these arguments have no weight whatever against the unanswerable contention that the present exclusion of women from the House of Deputies represents a fundamental denial of democratic rights and makes a mockery of the Church's claim that its government is based upon representative principles. To deny a diocese the right to choose the most capable of its members to represent it in the General Con-

vention on the basis of suppositions about the inferiority
or inadequacy of women to fulfill such responsibilities flies
in the face of all logic and all reason.

Surely this anomalous situation cannot long continue.
It is surely no part of the genius of Anglicanism, since in
almost every other branch of the Anglican Communion
women have full and equal rights of participation in
the democratic assemblies that the constitutions of those
churches provide. Incidentally, the retort of some critics to
these arguments that they might be equally advanced in
favor of the ordination to women to the priesthood is a point
well taken. Only a long tradition, based upon social patterns which barred women from participation in many
elements of public life, supports the present policy of an
exclusively male ministry. Admittedly, however, the ac-
complishment of this change is much farther away, and
the delay may be defended on the pragmatic ground that
probably very few congregations of the Episcopal Church
would be prepared to accept the ministrations of a woman
priest. This, however, is admittedly only another way of
saying that the traditional role of the sexes is rather deeply
fixed in our Church patterns and that change, even though
it may have logic in its favor, will come only slowly.

A number of other women's organizations, of course,
exist within the general framework of the Woman's Auxiliary, and in many places independent women's organizations have grown up. The Daughters of the King, as an
example of the former, is a well established and widely
useful organization, stressing the development of the spiritual life of women and of personal service to the rector
and parish. The Church Periodical Club is another organ-

ization of established reputation and wide usefulness, having as its objective the distribution of religious periodicals and literature. Time fails to mention the many clubs, guilds, circles and leagues by which the women of the Episcopal Church express their loving loyalty to Christ and their fellowship one with another.

The men of the Church have never matched the women in the efficiency of their organization nor the dramatic character of their service and contribution to the Church's life and program. Only since 1942 has there been any attempt to organize the work of the men of the Church on a nation-wide and church-wide scale. It has taken the form of the Presiding Bishop's Committee on Laymen's Work. Undoubtedly it has contributed enormously to raising the level of interest and organized activity among the men of the Church, but the truth is that it has not so far begun to realize its full potentialities. I have had the privilege of leading diocesan laymen's conferences in places as widely separated as Maine and Texas, and one is gratified to report a great eagerness to learn more about the Church's life and her ways and her faith and to devise methods by which men can serve the Church more effectively. Too often in the past the typical men's club dinner was a thinly disguised and slightly "churchy" version of the sessions of a local service club. A typical program would consist of invocation by the rector (oftentimes the single distinctively Christian activity of the evening), a high-calorie dinner (served, of course, by members of the Woman's Auxiliary), some community singing (perhaps some overly pious member would insist on including a hymn or two), and a rousing

talk by a local orator on "Trout Fishing in the Upper
Adirondacks," sometimes accompanied by colored slides!

Such programs might be harmless enough if it were not
for the fact that large areas of a man's world are today
demanding analysis and understanding in terms of his religious faith and outlook. What is the role of Christian
ethics, for example, in the conduct of American business?
Obviously, this is not a question which the average clergyman will be able to do very much to illuminate. He lives,
for the most part, above the struggle for business survival
and success and with the best will in the world must very
largely leave this question to the prayerful thinking of the
men of the Church. To ask men to discuss these questions,
however, is usually to be met by a blank uncomprehending
look or an unconvincing set of platitudes. A vigorous
group of clergy and business men continues to try to per-
suade the Christian Church as a whole that Adam Smith's
laissez-faire theories of economics are the only views consistent with Biblical faith. One must honor them for at
least making the effort to speak about business life in terms
of some pattern of philosophic or religious meaning. The
truth is that the ethical tradition of the Church has a
great deal to say about the meaning of Christianity in
economic and business life, and it is therefore something
of a tragedy that all those talks about "trout fishing in the
Adirondacks" should be taking up so much valuable time.
Like the women, men are often tempted to express their
devotion to the Church by the performance of practical
but essentially menial tasks. They supervise, in many cases,
the buildings and grounds of the parish, its finances, its

publicity, and they give their services gladly as ushers, choir members, participants in the Every Member Canvass and in many other useful and practical ways. Until the national organization of laymen, however, is able to do what the Woman's Auxiliary has done in turning the attention of church people to matters of worship and study, they will have failed even to begin to face up to their responsibilities.

The Episcopal Church's work with children and young people deserves a chapter to itself. To complete our picture, however, we need to refer to the growing development of small study groups, often drawn together as young married couples, meeting in the homes of some members. Such a young married people's group was one of the most promising developments in my early ministry, and it is rewarding to see how members of that small group are now serving as wardens, vestrymen, Woman's Auxiliary presidents, and in a number of other useful ways in places in the Church. I have always believed that a young person at the time of marriage, with the coming of young children and the assumption of the responsibilities of establishing a home, getting started in one's life work, and the other important undertakings that characterize that period of a person's life, is in a specially receptive mood to think about religion.

Much less widespread is the existence of special activities for elderly people within the fellowship of the Church. So far as I am informed, the Methodist Church mut be given the credit for having done more in this field than any other Christian body. However, here and there in the Episcopal Church groups of senior citizens are being drawn together, reflecting the obvious fact that in our society the number of elderly people is increasing and that because of developments in medical science they are living on with extraordinary vigor and energy. Any organized program for elderly people needs, however, special wisdom and preparation, and until more attention is given to these matters in pastoral theology in our seminaries the program will not realize its full possibilities.

Perhaps the highest expression of the possibilities of Christian community are realized in what has been traditionally known as the "religious life." Many people, including life-long Episcopalians, frequently ask in open-mouthed astonishment, "Does the Episcopal Church have monks and nuns?" The answer, of course, is that we do. Protestant prejudice against Religious Orders is probably attributable in large part to the prejudice of Martin Luther. For him monasticism was a denial of the Gospel and of the Christian view of the world. He felt strongly about it, because the monasticism he had known seemed to suggest to him that it was in the multiplication of special acts of devotion and in the performance of the special vows of the monastic that one gained God's favor and earned God's forgiveness. Luther also reacted strongly against the implied disparagement of marriage which he thought monasticism involved. For whatever reasons, he condemned monasticism as a wholly unwarranted Christian vocation, and Protestantism generally followed his lead. Even Henry VIII, who was by no means a follower of Lutheran ideas as a rule, suppressed the monastic orders in England and with the proceeds of this expropriation of

funds and properties created most of the titled nobility to
be found in contemporary England.

Except for a few scattered attempts to revive the monastic life in modified form of which the experiment at Little
Gidding in the Seventeenth Century was a peculiarly attractive example, Anglicanism knew nothing of monasticism
until the Oxford Movement of the 1830's and 1840's. As a
part of the new interest in church traditions of the past, the
Anglo-Catholics encouraged the re-establishment of Anglican monastic orders. Naturally this movement soon spread
to the Episcopal Church in the United States. Father James
Huntington, for example, persuaded Bishop Potter of New
York to receive his profession of vows as a novice and thus
establish the Order of the Holy Cross on November 25,
1884. Although the public outcry was considerable and
sharply critical both of Father Huntington and Bishop
Potter, the Order nevertheless grew and prospered and remains today one of the leading communities for men in the
Episcopal Church. My own experience both with the Order
of the Holy Cross and with the Sisters of the Holy Nativity
and the Sisters of the Transfiguration—to name the religious orders of which I have had personal experience—leads
me to the conviction that they are mainly free from the as-
sumptions that offended Luther and that a reformed monasticism is as conceivable as the reformation of any other
aspect of the Christian tradition. At its best, monasticism
may represent a desire of men and women to take upon
themselves, as Bishop Potter expressed it in defense of his
actions in receiving Father Huntington's vows, "the soldier
life and the soldier rule, turning their backs on home and

gain in a self-directed life ... Is poverty inconsistent with
the Christian calling? Is the unmarried state? Is obedience to a daily rule of prayer and work?" Bishop Potter
went on to voice the hope that the Order of the Holy Cross,
and by inference other monastic orders both for men and
women that might be established, "might do a John the
Baptist work." The life of the religious communities remains one of the least known aspects of the life of the
Episcopal Church, and yet it has a potential attraction for
many men and women who would respond to the challenge
and discipline that it involves. Certainly for the Church
to have before its eyes the spectacle of a company of men
and women who have renounced worldly positions, the
normal satisfactions of marriage and family life and the
privilege of self-direction and absolute liberty of choice,
not because they think these things inherently wicked in
themselves but that they are willing to renounce them in
order to be free to serve God in special circumstances and
special ways, is surely a healthy thing in an age when the
Church is too easily beguiled by the ways of the world and
too readily adapts its rigorous ethic to whatever is comfortable and fashionable.

So I am an Episcopalian in large part because I have
known other Episcopalians. They have invited me, welcomed me, instructed me, inspired me, and as a fellowship
of people, more united by their common acceptance of
Christ's forgiveness and their common acceptance of responsibility as His disciples than by natural affinity or con-
geniality, they have shown me something of what St. Paul
meant by "the Body of Christ." I do not say, of course, that
they have not often irritated me, dismayed me, appalled

me, and even sometimes bored me! But since I must have often created the same impression on them, perhaps it is just another way of demonstrating the profundity and strength of our fellowship one with another.

ELEVEN

"TAKE HEED THAT
THIS CHILD LEARN"

VERY EARLY in my experience at the Episcopal
Church I saw that they took seriously the question of
Christian education. Before I could become an Episcopalian I was required to attend a series of classes and to
study carefully the Prayer Book and the Catechism. My
present recollections of that instruction are very hazy, but
the fact that I can remember the rector's remarks about
evolution and the doctrine of creation as stated in the
Creed is, I think, evidence enough of his ability to communicate to a 13-year old boy. Perhaps even more lasting
and impressive was the training I received in connection
with membership in the boys' choir and later on as an
acolyte. To take part, Sunday after Sunday, in the worship
of the Church meant, of course, gaining some knowledge of
the meaning of the seasons of the Church Year, the usage
of the Prayer Book, the significance of certain ceremonial
postures and gestures, and a great many other things which

initiated me rapidly into the Episcopal Church and gave me the comfortable and smug feeling of being an insider on something quite impressive and important.

In its emphasis upon Confirmation, the Church obviously is expressing her high estimation of the importance of instruction and education in preparation for the Christian life. The outline of the subjects to be treated is implied in the form of the Catechism. In most parishes a Confirmation date is established with the Bishop, and preparations begin many weeks before to recruit and train a class for presentation to him. Many who are already confirmed take advantage of these annual classes to refresh their own memory of the Church's teachings. The following list suggests the range of topics that are usually covered in such instructions: the Church's theological teachings, her attitude toward the Bible, the Creeds, tradition, reason; Church history, a sketch of the development of Christianity since our Lord's Resurrection and Ascension, the origin and development of the Church of England, the early days of the Episcopal Church in America, the crisis of the Revolution, and its subsequent growth; the Church's ethical teachings, the Christian meaning of marriage and her attitude toward divorce, her discipline of fasting and penitence, the obligations of the laity with respect to church attendance and church support, the Church's teaching about society and its relationship to the world; the Church's government, its organization, the doctrine of the ministry, highlights of the Church's canon law; the missionary program of the Church, the rights and responsibilities of the laity in Church government; the Church's worship, the principles of liturgical worship, the structure

and meaning of the choir offices and the occasional offices,
ceremonial customs, the Church Year, the meaning of
vestments and church ornaments; the Holy Communion,
its meaning and place in the Christian life, doctrines of
the presence of Christ in the Holy Communion, preparation for the Holy Communion, ceremonial practices and
customs having to do with its observance.

In addition to this rather full outline, I have always
made it a practice to introduce members of the Confirmation class to the life of the particular parish into which
they are coming by Confirmation. Representatives of
parish organizations explain and describe the various func-
tionings of parochial life. In addition to children who are
presented for Confirmation in fulfillment of their baptismal vows, there are always, of course, many adults, most
of them with some previous religious connections who for
one reason or another are seeking to know more about the
Episcopal Church and on the basis of what they discover
seeking to be confirmed members of it. In every parish
in which I have ever served, the Confirmation classes presented to the Bishop contained almost always as many or
more adults than children. In one case an advertisement
inserted for only one Saturday in a metropolitan news-
paper with the heading "Why Not Be An Episcopalian?"
brought nearly 150 people to the first meeting of the class.
The title of the ad sounds a little brash as I look back on
it, and as a bishop who saw it exclaimed, "Well, why not?"
But the results obviously show that a great many people
in that metropolitan area were seeking some religious
affiliation and were ready to respond to an invitation to

find out something about one of the main traditions of Christendom.

In theory, the provision for Confirmation instruction is a way of demonstrating the Church's concern that her membership shall be an informed one. Unfortunately all too often Confirmation instruction is attended only sporadically, and many children learn enough to make a satisfactory showing on an examination but retain very little of the specific instruction in later life. Every Episcopal clergyman is distressed by the lack of information that is all too evident even in some of his most devoted people. The Christian view of history implies that learning about things having to do with God and His Church can have no end, for new situations are always arising in which the meaning and relevance of the Christian faith must be freshly discovered and applied. Much has been said about the religious illiteracy of our time, and the Episcopal Church has had its full share. The experience of military chaplains in the Second World War indicated the shocking ignorance on the part of people of all churches, or of none, about the most elementary matters having to do with the Bible and the Christian faith. Miss Dorothy Sayers has paraphrased the average Englishman's reaction, for example, to the doctrine of the Trinity, imaging him as muttering over the words of the Athanasian Creed (a Creed which is not found in the American Prayer Book), "the Father incomprehensible, the Son incomprehensible, the Holy Ghost incomprehensible . . . the whole thing incomprehensible!" So, many people have regarded the fundamental doctrines of the Christian faith, and against such widespread ignorance and even lack of interest, a few sessions of a Confirmation

class are, of course, woefully inadequate as preparation for
a thorough understanding and grounding in Christian
knowledge.

What about the Sunday School? I had very little experience as a pupil in the Episcopal Sunday School, but I
spent several exciting years as a teacher. Until fairly recently the Episcopal Church has made no effort to provide
an official curriculum for its Sunday Schools. Partly as a
result of the widespread ignorance of the Christian faith
discovered by military chaplains in the war, the General
Convention of 1946 authorized a great expansion of the
Department of Christian Education with the specific au-
thorization for the Department to proceed to the development of an official curriculum. Few tasks in the history of
the Church have ever been undertaken with more thor-
oughness or greater statesmanship. The primary responsibility was vested in the Rev. John Heuss, D.D., now rector
of Trinity Parish in New York City. Dr. Heuss wisely
realized that the task of Christian education was a far more
complex one than simply writing out a series of study
guides for Sunday School classes. The Church needed, in
his opinion, to reconsider its whole educational task and
philosophy and to grasp the truth which is at the heart of
much progressive and modern educational theory, mainly
that a person learns best when he is interested and that
he is interested when the material seems to have some
relevance to his own needs and situation.

Fortunately much of this philosophy had already been
suggested to me in my experiences as a Church Sunday
School teacher which the reader has heard of in the first
chapter of this book. It was a Sunday School in which

great stress was laid upon the totality of learning which took place within the whole experience of the Sunday School period. Habits of reverence and worship in church, habits of thoughtfulness and consideration in class—these counted for just as much as the amount of information acquired. On the other hand, this was no faddism, which suggested that the intellectual content of the Christian tradition was of no importance. The natural interest and skills of children were, however, enlisted for the learning process. One of the most spectacular results was a great relief map of Palestine, created by a class of fourth-grade boys who were led by their patient teacher beyond the stage of throwing pellets of paper pulp at each other to the more constructive experience of grasping the nature and terrain of the Holy Land and presenting it graphically and artistically by means of paper pulp on a great sheet of plywood. I am willing to wager that if one of those boys now were asked what he knew about the topography of the Holy Land, the answers would be astonishing in their competence.

The problem of the Sunday School remains, however, an extraordinarily difficult one. The problem of providing, for example, for suitable space, properly equipped, for the purpose of teaching children for only one or two hours a week is a staggering economic problem just in itself. Trained and competent teachers are, of course, few and far between and notoriously difficult to pin down to a regular Sunday after Sunday responsibility. It has been estimated that children enrolled in Sunday School are usually absent about forty per cent of the time. What would the public schools be able to do with an attendance record as poor as that? All that one can claim for the Episcopal Church is that it has tried to face these problems in the development of its new curriculum and has made some promising suggestions, looking toward a solution. Parents, for example, are to be deeply involved in the whole teaching process. Many parts of the curriculum require the active participation of parents working with the child in the home. Considerable flexibility is allowed in the use of materials, leaving the teacher free to adopt classroom procedures suitable to the wide variety of situations with which he or she may be confronted. The new Episcopal Church curriculum, usually called the Seabury Series, is, of course, only in an experimental stage. It has reached its final form for publication only in the last four or five years, and consequently I myself have never had the responsibility of using it, since my duties as a university chaplain do not include the supervision of a Sunday School. Discussions and comments throughout the Church suggest, however, that a great deal remains to be accomplished before the Seabury Series will have achieved a form which will commend it to the overwhelming majority of the Church. Developments up to the present indicate, however, several important things about the Episcopal Church's attitude toward the task of educating her children. In the first place, she regards education as a far more profound development than the acquisition of information. In the second place, she believes that the Christian faith can best be understood in terms of the real life situations in which boys and girls and men and women find themselves. In the third place, she recognizes the role of the family and the Christian home as a teaching agency. Fourthly, she has set an admittedly high standard for teachers and demanded a generous investment of time and money on the part of the parish and of its leadership for the educational task. Dr. Heuss and his successor, the Rev. David M. Hunter, deserve the Church's grateful thanks for setting these principles so clearly before us and moving to put them to work.

One of the important means for Christian education is the extensive program which the Episcopal Church carries on in elementary and secondary education, traditionally in select boarding schools but increasingly through the use of a parochial school system. In the Diocese of Los Angeles, for example, eleven parish day schools have been developed in the last twelve years. High standards are maintained by the diligent supervision of a Department of Parish Day Schools, established as a part of the diocesan administration. Other parts of the country have seen equally spectacular developments in many places and the Episcopal Church may be on the verge of discovering an important new solution for the problem of the training of her children. It would be unfortunate, of course, if this development involved any loss of interest in maintaining the quality of publicly supported education in the communities of America. The troublesome problems that arise, however, in dealing with religion in the public schools under the usual interpretation that has prevailed of the meaning of the principle of the separation of Church and State have limited the effectiveness of the public schools in the eyes of many church people. There is much to provoke thought in the observation of the late Archbishop Temple of Canterbury that one can not omit from the education that goes on five days in the week all mention

of God and then suddenly introduce Him for one hour on
Sunday without suggesting that He is essentially irrelevant
to the whole business of life! Many thorny problems
bristle in this area, but at least the Episcopal Church's deep
concern for the religious training of her children is evident
in the vigorous provision she is making through the parochial school program.

The parochial schools, of course, are simply carrying
further an interest in secondary education that has always
been characteristic of the Episcopal Church, especially in
its long-established centres. Under more or less direct
church auspices hundreds of secondary and preparatory
schools are carrying on programs throughout the United
States. Some of them like Groton, St. Paul's, Kent and
Choate have famous and enviable reputations. Their contribution to the vigor and life of the Episcopal Church
cannot be questioned. Although the religious interests of
another generation differ very considerably from our own,
one cannot deny the influence for good exerted by an
Endicott Peabody of Groton or a Samuel S. Drury of
St. Paul's. A recent biographer of Franklin Delano Roosevelt, a Groton graduate who was conspicuously devoted to
Endicott Peabody, writes, for example, about Roosevelt:
"He believed in doing good, in showing other people how
to do good, and he assumed that ultimately people would
do good. By 'good' he meant the Ten Commandments and
the Golden Rule, as interpreted by Endicott Peabody." *
On the other hand, the same biographer cites Roosevelt's
inaugural address, delivered just before he left for the Yalta

* Burns, James MacGregor: *Roosevelt, The Lion and the Fox.* Harcourt,
Brace. 1956. Page 475.

Conference, in which he quoted Peabody as saying that "the great fact to remember is that the trend of civilization itself is forever upward; that a line drawn through the middle of the peaks and the valleys of the centuries always has an upward trend." ** Obviously such a view of the inevitable progress of history is more a consequence of the general optimism of the late 19th and early 20th centuries than it is a result of any serious reading of the Bible. If President Roosevelt may be considered a typical Episcopalian, his attitude toward Christian education may give cause for widespread alarm. When his wife raised with him the question of the religious upbringing of the children, "he said simply that they should go to church and learn what he had learned. 'But are you sure that you believe in everything you learned?' his wife persisted. 'I really never thought about it,' he said with a quizzical look. 'I think it is just as well not to think about things like that.' " ***

If Groton taught Franklin Roosevelt a deep loyalty to his Church, it obviously taught him something important. But if it taught him that religion is to be accepted without question and that everything is moving steadily and automatically toward perfection, then it seriously misled him. But, of course, the theological revolution of the third and fourth decades of this century has left its mark also upon the Episcopal Church's secondary schools, and there is increasing evidence of a willingness to wrestle with deep questions of theology and their relevance to the responsibilities of secondary education. The provision of an ad-

** *Ibid*, page 470.
*** *Ibid*, page 475.

ministrative officer in the Department of Christian Education as a full-time consultant on church preparatory schools is welcome evidence that the Episcopal Church intends to take more seriously in the future than it has in the past the theological content of its program of Christian education in these strategic institutions.

The reader will not be surprised in view of my present position in the Church to hear that I believe that one of the great opportunities before the Episcopal Church and one in which it is realizing ever more fully its possibilities is the whole field of work on the campuses of our colleges and universities. Surprisingly enough, in view of the prominence which the universities of Cambridge and Oxford played in the history of the Church of England, very few Anglican institutions of higher learning in America survive to the present day. Only the University of the South, at Sewanee, Tennessee, Kenyon College at Gambier, Ohio, Trinity College at Hartford, Connecticut, and the Colleges of the Seneca at Geneva, New York, continue today as accredited institutions of higher learning directly under the sponsorship and control of the Episcopal Church. Several colonial colleges, notably Columbia University and the College of William and Mary, had Anglican influences in their beginnings and early history, but no direct control by the Episcopal Church is provided for at the present time.

The Church's record of work in universities and colleges, however, blossomed in vigorous development after the First World War. Leslie Glenn and Fred Kellogg at Harvard, John Crocker at Princeton, Arthur L. Kinsolving at Amherst, Brooke Stabler at Pennsylvania—these were some of the great names of the early days of the ministry of the Episcopal Church to the college campus. Much of the enthusiasm for this work is due to the pioneering labors of the Church Society for College Work and the willingness of a few clergy and laity of broad vision to make the college ministry a matter of high priority. Part of the reason, of course, was that the percentage of Episcopal students in colleges far exceeded—in some cases more than double—the percentage of Episcopalians in the population as a whole. As some wag observed, "Episcopalians are denser in colleges than elsewhere."

In its earlier days, it is perhaps not unfair to say that the main preoccupation of the college chaplain to Episcopal students was to retain their loyalty to the Church or to convert outsiders to the Church against the unfavorable tide of thinking and opinion which characterized the campus as a whole. Due in large part, however, to the growing concern of the college chaplain with Episcopal faculty personnel, this tendency has shown a gradual change of direction. It is now recognized that Anglican theology gives the character of divine vocation to the scholarly pursuit of the campus and that the Episcopal Church's ministry, therefore, is not only to rescue people out of their academic world but to transform their whole outlook upon their academic work. The Christian faith, after all, is in the God of creation, the God who moves and works in nature and in history. Every genuine discovery of truth must, therefore, be seen as a new revelation of the character and mind of God. All learning is potentially theological in its meaning. One of the main responsibilities of the Episcopal Church's ministry to the campus is to make this truth clear.

The revival of religious studies in the contemporary American college and university is an unmistakable sign of the times. Departments and courses in religion are springing up on all sides. At Columbia University, for example, under the vigorous chaplaincy of James A. Pike, a full department of religion was organized and the offerings of courses were increased from four or five to some twenty-five or thirty. This burgeoning growth represents an enormous opportunity for the Church. Especially to an Episcopalian, with his background of a tradition of religious humanism and of the validity of man's reason as one of the ways in which he can know God, the scholarly study of religion, marked by the same sharpness of inquiry and rigor of method which is found in any other of the academic disciplines, can help create a well-informed and theologically articulate laity.

A generation ago the hope was held forth that by the Episcopal Church's ministry to the campus it could save a few college students for the Church. Now the possibility is dawning that the ministry of the Episcopal Church on the college and university campus may, as a matter of fact, save the Church itself by raising it to new levels of relevance and self-awareness. It would not, of course, be the first time in church history that the Church's life had been revitalized from the college campus or its equivalent. The Lutheran Reformation began at a university, so did the Evangelical Revival, so did the Tractarian Movement of the 1830's. Is it too much to hope that the predominance of theological interest on the contemporary college campus, the great attention given to theologians like Reinhold Niebuhr and Paul Tillich, will bring new theological

sharpness and clarity to our churches through the young
men and women who graduate from our universities and
colleges in these next few years? Fortunately the vigor and
vitality of the Episcopal Church's ministry to the college
campus puts it in a strategic position to make maximum
use of this new development.

Only slowly is the Episcopal Church beginning to realize
the possibilities of teaching her faith and demonstrating
the quality of her life by means of some of the new techniques of mass communication. The eagerness with which
television networks, for example, are prepared to telecast
some of the services of the great seasons of the Church
Year from important church centres suggests that there is
an opportunity that will soon have to be taken with new
seriousness. The pioneering work of Dean James A. Pike,
of the New York Cathedral, through his weekly television
program suggests a format which while not obtrusively
Episcopalian in form and character nevertheless has important things to say and impressions to create which illuminate greatly the genius and character of the Episcopal
Church. "May his tribe increase." The same opportunity
would appear to exist in the realm of religious books. In
England, for a long time the work of such Anglicans as
C. S. Lewis and Dorothy Sayers has reached a wide audience. Among American Episcopalians none has achieved
quite the eminence of their English counterparts, but
writers like Dean Pike, Professor Chad Walsh of Beloit
College, Professors Norman Pittenger and J. V. Langmead
Casserley of the General Theological Seminary, Bishop
Angus Dun of Washington, Professor William J. Wolf of
the Episcopal Theological School at Cambridge—give

promise of seizing for the Episcopal Church the opportunity represented in the present revival of interest in
religion and the corresponding rising tide of sales of religious books.

The enormous educational task that rests upon the
modern clergyman points, of course, to the importance of
a well-trained ministry and to the strategic role which the
seminaries and divinity schools of the Church will play in
shaping its future. Since the Second World War the number of candidates for the ministry has multiplied impressively, although the number still falls short of those needed
to maintain the present work of the Church and provide
for new developments. It is a tribute, however, to the
seriousness with which the Episcopal Church regards the
importance of an educated ministry that despite the in-
sistent clamor for more clergy and the consequent temptation to lower standards and to condone short-cuts in training, by and large the standards for the training of the
clergy have remained high.

Unlike most other religious bodies, the Episcopal
Church does not assume any official responsibility for the
support or the standards of its theological training schools.
Only the General Theological Seminary in New York City
has any relationship whatever to the General Convention,
and this relationship is a very limited one whereby the
Convention elects certain members of the Board of Trus-
tees and the Seminary makes a report every three years to
the Convention. Some other seminaries have a similar connection with a diocese or with a group of dioceses or in
some cases with the Provincial Synod. A Joint Commission
of the General Convention on Theological Education has

existed for several years, and it extends or withholds a quasi-official recognition of a theological seminary according to whether it meets the minimum standards of the American Association of Theological Schools. A seminary, however, which does not meet the standards is nevertheless perfectly free to continue to exist as long as it can recruit a faculty and student body. Given the different traditions and schools of thought which are represented within the Episcopal Church, this *laissez faire* attitude toward theological education is perhaps inevitable and may provide a salutary kind of competition and specialization. Many Episcopalians feel, however, that the Church ought to take official cognizance of the seminaries in a more thoroughgoing way than is now the case, setting standards and guaranteeing adequate support.

The ultimate responsibility for determining the adequacy of the preparation of a candidate for the ministry is left up to the bishop of his diocese and the board of examining chaplains. The young candidate for ordination often complains about this system and about the difficulty of following up his preparation for the successful completion of his seminary course with another preparation—which may be very different in character—for passing the examinations of the examining chaplains of his own diocese. As all students know, the passing of examinations is an art, consisting partly in a sensitivity to the prejudices and peculiarities of the examiners! Perhaps it is asking a great deal of a young candidate for Holy Orders to expect him to learn the peculiarities of his seminary faculty and then in addition to that have to learn the peculiarities of his bishop and board of examining chaplains.

I remember two questions, for example, in my own examinations, one by a distinguished elderly clergyman who had the pessimistic view that "they don't teach the Bible any more in the seminaries." His question in the examination in the Old Testament was to recount the narrative portions of the first five chapters of the Second Book of Samuel! This obviously required not only a knowledge of the story of King David but also enough familiarity with the chapter arrangements to know what parts of the account fall within the first five chapters of II Samuel. To my amazement I seemed to have guessed with fair accuracy, and was pronounced by the elderly examiner to be one of the most learned men in the Old Testament that it had been his privilege to examine in many a long day! Another questioner wanted to know the "philosophy"—and I think that is the exact word he used—which lay behind the custom of lighting the candle on the right, or the "epistle" side, of the altar first, and the light on the left, or "gospel" side, of the altar, second and extinguishing them in the reverse order. I had no idea of the answer, and although he impressed upon me the great importance of being prepared to answer what may seem trivial questions from parishioners, I found to my surprise that he didn't seem to have a very good answer either. Friends of mine from another diocese exchanged horror stories about the rumors current about one of their examining chaplains, who wanted to know "how many Wise Men visited the Infant Jesus?" If any one presumed to answer "three," he would roar at them, "where do you find that in the Gospels?" He would then triumphantly demonstrate that the story in St. Matthew mentions only "wise men" and only the

three-fold gifts of gold, frankincense and myrrh has led to
the assumption that the number of wise men was actually
three. These sample questions are not intended to deride
the provision for examining chaplains. It is probably de-
sirable, as long as the Church takes so little official interest
in the curriculum of the seminaries, that an independent
examination in each diocese test the range and adequacy
of the candidate's preparation. Efforts are being made to
standardize examinations to some extent and to correlate
the demands of examining chaplains with the preparation
in the seminary. This is a consummation devoutly to be
hoped for by any clergyman who has either taken or given
canonical examinations—and that presumably includes all
of them.

By and large the seminaries give thorough consideration
to the great areas of theological study: the Old and New
Testaments, church history, systematic theology, pastoral
theology, liturgics, canon law, Christian ethics and moral
theology, and Christian education. If any criticism can be
made of the seminaries and divinity schools of the Church,
perhaps this one is the most justifiable, that they carry on
their instruction too much in isolation from the main intellectual currents of the world around them. Some of the
seminaries by reason of geographical location are cut off
from contact with a great university. Others, however,
although located in reasonable proximity to such a university, seem to take very little advantage of the possibilities which such proximity suggests. Too little effort is made
in the seminary to relate the interests that a student has
developed in his undergraduate studies to his theological
training. This of course is no doubt due in part to the wide

diversity of undergraduate preparation which a typical seminary student body represents. Some seminaries include courses in "apologetics" or in "the philosophy of religion." In so far as such courses examine the cultural and intellectual tendencies of our modern world and show the points of similarity and contrast between these tendencies and the presuppositions of the Christian's world outlook, they are fulfilling the kind of requirement that I have in mind. Would it not, however, enrich and make more exciting the program both of the seminary and of the secular university to have the two confronting each other from time to time on a scholarly level, debating, differing, agreeing but even under the most unfavorable circumstances facilitating to some extent communication between theology and other intellectual interests of our time?

Most of the seminaries of the Episcopal Church, of course, concentrate upon the training of men for the parochial ministry. Few of them provide opportunities for doing advanced scholarly work in the theological studies. In contrast to generous scholarship programs that exist in some other denominations and communions to encourage promising students to go on to gain advanced degrees in some of the great graduate schools of theology in America and abroad, the Episcopal Church lags far behind and may find herself woefully under-supplied—if she has not indeed already found herself so—with men competent in theological scholarship and teaching. Inquiries come to me with great frequency from men and women who are asking for help in finding ways to undertake a program of graduate study with meagre financial resources and in many cases the responsibility of a family to be considered.

Only a fraction, the more fortunate, are able to realize their ambition. For a Church that has insisted on an educated and learned ministry, the Episcopal Church has done shockingly little to make possible the realization of that ideal.

Two institutions for the training of women workers in the Episcopal Church exist, St. Margaret's House in Berkeley, California, and Windham House in New York City. Despite the uncertainty which exists within the Church as to just how such women workers are to be used and what responsibilities they are to have, both institutions have a creditable record for providing the Church with competent professional women workers serving as directors of religious education, workers on college campuses, workers in church social service agencies, etc. Studies are going on as this is being written to help to regularize and clarify the status of women workers in the Episcopal Church—a long overdue step which ought to increase the number of candidates and insure a more effective use of their talents and abilities.

The Episcopal Church obviously gives high significance to education—both for her children, her young people, her adults and her clergy and other full-time professional workers. As we have seen in another chapter, this educational enterprise is allowed to go on without the restrictions of an excessive dogmatism or a Biblical liberalism but rather on the assumption that the consecrated use of one's intellectual abilities is a justifiable way in which to serve and glorify God. This respect for education is one of the truly impressive characteristics of the Episcopal Church and one in which I have always rejoiced.

TWELVE

"WE HAVE ERRED AND STRAYED"

I HOPE I have not portrayed the Episcopal Church in too generous and rosy a light. As I look back over the preceding chapters the predominant note has been gratitude for the many ways in which this Church to which I came as a stranger more than thirty years ago has fulfilled for me the ideals of a Christian community and the Body of Christ. It would not be true, of course, to say that the Episcopal Church always makes me proud of my decision to come into its membership and to enter its ministry. It is easy to think of faults—some of them very serious—about which anyone considering the Episcopal Church as a spiritual home ought to be warned lest he find himself disillusioned. One ought to be realistic, for example, about our support of the foreign missionary enterprise. It is disgracefully inadequate. Of all the money received from her people the Episcopal Church devotes only about five per cent to the program of the National Church—and that includes Christian Education, Christian Social Relations, and many other activities in addition to the support for foreign missions. Episcopalians give on a per capita basis less than four dollars a year to the whole program of the National Church. I am not proud of that record. Something is terribly wrong with the sense of values of a Church that lets the great world opportunities of this mid-Twentieth Century go by without seizing them in the name of Christ, and all because we spend more than ninety-five per cent of our gifts and offerings on our own churches and within our own national boundaries. It is embarrassing to report that Episcopalians are among the worst religious and ecclesiastical isolationists in Christendom.

I am not proud either of the attitude of many Episcopalians about cooperative Christianity. As president of a metropolitan Church Federation I found myself almost alone in my support of its program. (Only about five or six Episcopal churches out of a total of 38 in the area served gave even token financial support to our work.) A kind of ecclesiastical snobbishness seems to pervade the Episcopal Church—not blatant and overt as a rule—but operating quietly to frustrate any real commitment to cooperative undertakings. There is a bland assumption that, as a testy old 18th Century gentleman is reported to have said, "There may be other ways to be a Christian than in the Episcopal Church, but no gentleman would take advantage of them"! As a Church we have done as much as any other body—and much more than most—for the sake of the Ecumenical Movement, but it remains on the level of top-echelon theological discussion and has no real support in the local communities. The difficulties of such local cooperation have already been described. The Episcopal Church represents an appreciation of tradition in an American ecclesiastical world where all history between the New Testament and the landing of the Pilgrims is too often considered fairly irrelevant. It stands for an authoritative ministry among churches that are highly independent and congregational in their conception of government and authority. It has an understanding of Catholic life and faith that enables it to understand the great Roman Catholic Church in a way that baffles and irritates most Protestants. We are a minority among the Protestant family of Church traditions—although we can often find support from individual leaders and usually from Lutherans and "High-Church" Presbyterians. Without compromising for a moment our own position, we might, however, get into the movement for cooperative Protestantism with both feet and help to form and direct its development rather than deride it for its one-sidedness and its many mistakes. The smug assumption of all too many Episcopalians that the rest of the Protestant world will come to us eventually and that consequently we have no need to go out to meet them is pompous presumption—not to say blasphemy against the Holy Spirit. It is *not* one of the reasons I am an Episcopalian.

I am distressed also by a subtle pressure for conformity that is spreading in the Episcopal Church—as indeed it may also be in the secular society of contemporary America— which defines the traditional "Via Media" (Middle Way) of Anglicanism as being frozen on dead center. My friends know I love argument and debate, and perhaps I am only justifying and rationalizing my own taste for controversy

when I say that I believe in a much more vigorous inter-
change between the several schools of thought in the
Episcopal Church than now seems to be going on. The
Via Media, for me, is an indefinable line that shifts back
and forth in the continuing encounter of the Anglo-Catholic, the Evangelical and the Broad Churchman. There is
almost a conspiracy these days to hush up real controversy
on principles and issues. General Convention has become
so quiet and mild-mannered that reporters leap on the
slightest murmur of controversy to give interest to the dull
accounts they are obliged to file. I hope I am not pleading
for controversy just for controversy's sake, but I do believe
that the Episcopal Church is in danger of confusing the
unity and godly love which ought always to characterize
the Church with the kind of conformity and amiability
which is the mark of what we have learned to call the
"other-directed" society. It was not always thus. Some of
the great controversialists of the past would be most un-
comfortable today. It is no compliment to the intensity of
our devotion as Episcopalians to be told that we cannot
risk controversy and an honest opposition of convictions
for fear of rending the Church asunder. We like to think
of Anglicanism, sometimes, as a "bridge Church," linking
both Catholic and Reformed elements in the Christian
tradition. I am not sure my metaphor will serve me here,
but I would urge that the bridge needs to be firmly
anchored on both sides of the supposed chasm! That is to
say, I hope we may have a deeply convinced and well-
informed and highly articulate Catholic party as well as a
deeply convinced, well-informed and highly articulate
Evangelical party, so that we may be kept in the middle

way—not because we like the middle way but because the demands of truth and comprehensiveness keep us there. If we try to define some "Anglican line" we shall be false to history and our unique calling as a Church that has much to teach the ecumenical movement about the meaning of a Catholic and Reformed Church which can live in unity without demanding uniformity.

I am glad that we are called upon so regularly by the services of the Prayer Book to confess our sins—and not just our personal sins but our sins as a Church. When we say that we have "erred and strayed from thy ways like lost sheep," do we not mean that we have as a Church often missed God's calling to us, have ignored the summons He issues to imagination and service, have betrayed the comprehensive and self-forgetful love which called us into existence as His family? Only a Church which is humbly aware of its shortcomings can possibly serve to mediate the love of God to the world and so justify its characterization as "the Body of Christ." The penitent Church is the best witness to the truth that it is the Holy and Living God whom we serve. The fact of our humility proves that we have some genuine knowledge of God Himself and have not bowed ourselves before an idol of our own contriving.

So a catalog of failings which can be compiled for the Episcopal Church does not dismay me—although I feel the shame and the rebuke of missed opportunities and wasted potentialities. In my disappointment and resentment, I can remember that the Episcopal Church itself has taught me the real meaning of what a Church ought to be, and that I am using the standard of the Prayer Book and the

Creeds and the Holy Scripture—all of which I know through the Episcopal Church—to call the Episcopal Church into judgment!

By the grace of God, I am also moved oftentimes to reflect that I have failed the Episcopal Church more times than she has failed me, that she corrects my prejudices and onesidedness, that she steadies my devotion which waxes and wanes with disturbing frequency, that she both rebukes and forgives my sloth and self-indulgence, that she holds before me always a goal of perfection—"that the rest of our life may be pure and holy"—which eludes me perennially but which calls to something deep within me which I am confident cannot forever be denied, that she points me forward to those good things that "pass man's understanding ... which God has prepared for those who unfeignedly love Him." One criticizes a Church that has meant so much to him only that it may speak more persuasively and winningly to others and play more effectively its all-important role in the economy of God for His Holy, Catholic and Apostolic Church which is being realized more fully in the ecumenical movement of our time. Without disparaging the witness and work of other branches of the Church, I can only bear testimony to my own discovery that in the Episcopal Church I found the most balanced, comprehensive, satisfying and stimulating experience of Christian faith and Christian life that I can imagine. I *became* an Episcopalian by a set of fortuitous circumstances, but I *am* an Episcopalian because in my experience I found there what it means to be a Christian.

INDEX

187